Life Lessons from Slasher Films

Jessica Robinson

THE SCARECROW PRESS, INC.
Lanham • Toronto • Plymouth, UK
2012

Published by Scarecrow Press, Inc.
A wholly owned subsidiary of The Rowman & Littlefield Publishing Group, Inc.
4501 Forbes Boulevard, Suite 200, Lanham, Maryland 20706
www.rowman.com

10 Thornbury Road, Plymouth PL6 7PP, United Kingdom

British Library Cataloguing in Publication Information Available

Library of Congress Cataloging-in-Publication Data

Robinson, Jessica, 1978–
 Life lessons from slasher films / Jessica Robinson.
  p. cm.
 Includes bibliographical references and index.
 ISBN 978-0-8108-8502-8 (cloth : alk. paper) — ISBN 978-0-8108-8503-5
(ebook)
 1. Slasher films—History and criticism. 2. Motion pictures—Social aspects.
I. Title.
 PN1995.9.S554R63 2012
 791.43'6164—dc23
                               2012008389

To Dax: I couldn't have written it without
your support and desire to get me interested in these films.

Thank you also to Bob Torry.
Without him, I wouldn't have received my master's
or had the courage to explore these ideas.

CONTENTS

PREFACE

I haven't always been a horror fan. I used to watch them when I was little, but it was always from between my fingers. It wasn't until I was in college that I developed a genuine interest in the genre. My husband was the first to get me excited about slasher films. His birthday is on the thirteenth, and it occasionally falls on a Friday, so he had a vested interest in the *Friday the 13th* films. We watched them for enjoyment, and it wasn't until I began working on my thesis that I looked at them with a discerning eye. I have always enjoyed slasher films, and no matter how many times I see them, parts still make me jump. When I started reading articles written about *Friday the 13th*, I found that a lot of authors believed these films were misogynistic and reinforced the ideas of patriarchy. The two greatest champions for these notions are Carol Clover and Vera Dika, who claim that women are objectified and picked on in these films just because they are women. They argue that women's deaths are lingered on longer than men's and that they are killed more often. They explain the Final Girl as being nothing more than an incredibly masculine female. But by looking at these films through the lens of feminism, important social commentary is disregarded. It irritated me that these authors dismissed the films because of antifeminist ideals, which aren't necessarily present. There were a few ideas Clover and Dika had that I agreed with. But mainly, their arguments made me want to figure out what these films were highlighting if it wasn't antiwomen sentiments.

This book is an extension of the work I did for my master's thesis. When I was trying to decide what to write, my first topic was to look at demons and their role in society. I wasn't quite sure which specific demons I wanted to look at, but I knew I wanted to do something with evil entities and their role throughout history. I was just getting into the genre of slasher films at the time, and my committee chair, Bob Torry, actually suggested that I write on the *Friday the 13th* films. I had seen them before, but I didn't really know what I was getting myself into.

INTRODUCTION

Slasher films are considered to be the bastard children of the horror film industry because of the content and techniques employed to make them. The original films rarely had a large budget to work with and were generally done by independent filmmakers. The violence in these movies was exceedingly graphic and has been readily picked apart and condemned by critics. Yet, despite all of these odds, the films have endured, and many of the originals were bought by large production companies because of the revenues they produced, and they have been remade within recent years to appeal to a whole new generation of moviegoers.

But what makes a slasher film?

In *Going to Pieces: The Rise and Fall of the Slasher Film, 1978–1986*, Adam Rockoff outlined seven basic elements that the films must incorporate in one form or another to be classified as a slasher. These include

1. An evil entity inflicting tragic deaths upon the characters

2. The killer's weapon of choice—a sharp, penetrating object, such as a butcher knife or machete

3. Graphic special effects to shock viewers

4. An isolated setting or location in which the intended victims are hunted and slaughtered

5. A traumatic event that triggers the killer's spree

6. A Final Girl who wages battle with the killer at the film's climax

7. The use of the killer's point of view

While not every slasher film features all of these elements, the majority of these can be found in most slasher films.

Every slasher film must have an evil entity inflicting tragic deaths upon the characters. Although the killer is usually a male, this is not always the case. In the very first *Friday the 13th*, the killer is a woman: Mrs. Voorhees, an upset mother who seeks revenge from the camp counselors who allowed her son, Jason, to drown (in the sequels, of course, Jason returns from the grave to inflict more carnage, taking up where his mother left off). The killer does not have to be indestructible, but in some way affected by a trauma, which becomes the motive for all of their murders. The killers are never depicted developing a plan for their murders, but kill "with systematic precision, uncaring, emotionless and unmerciful" (Rockoff 6). This, as Rockoff claims, classifies them as homicidal maniacs. They are usually more concerned with exacting revenge than they are with lingering on the victim's agony. The murders are usually quick and painless.

Rockoff envisions most killers as "epitomizing masculinity to ludicrous extremes" (6), and he also classifies the killer in most films as being asexual. Despite the overt sexuality that occurs in these films, the killer never participates in, or is incapable of participating in such acts. The killer has moments of voyeurism, but these usually occur right before a murder. The killer feels no pleasure during these peeping episodes, only the need to kill those within his gaze.

Rockoff's second category for these films is the killer's weapon of choice. As the label "slasher film" suggests, the victims are murdered with sharp, penetrating objects. Generally, a knife or machete is used, but objects such as spears, arrows, axes, or harpoons work just as well. Anything that pierces flesh is employed as a weapon. Occasionally, when such objects cannot be found, brute strength is used. These types of killings, unlike those in many action films that use guns, make the deaths much more personal for the audience and the killer. Both have to get close to the victim.

The third category in Rockoff's basic elements of slasher films deals with special effects. By the 1980s, special effects had grown by leaps and bounds, and the question was no longer what could be done but what could be shown. Rockoff claims that the work Tom Savini did on *Friday the 13th* had a huge impact on special effects for horror movies that were to follow. Many of the films that came before, such as *Psycho*, *The Texas Chain Saw Massacre*, and *Halloween*, relied more on audience imagination than visible gore. These films had very low budgets and could not afford realistic-looking blood or expensive makeup that looked like flesh being stabbed. Despite the violence of the shower scene in *Psycho*, the knife that does in the victims is never shown penetrating flesh. Many of the chain saw scenes that occur in *Texas* are done from behind a curtain, where the audience gets the implied cutting of bodies, but never actually sees it. In *Halloween*, the audience never sees a drop of blood being spilled.

Friday the 13th changed all of that.

Tom Savini's special effects allowed the audience to see all of the gruesome detail right in their face and in all its bloody horror. He designed the famous scene where Kevin Bacon's character, Jack, is stabbed from under the bed, the scene in which Marcie gets an ax in the face, and the final scene when Mrs. Voorhees is decapitated. The audience is also horrified to see a body pinned to a door by arrows. The deaths are shown in all of their gruesome, bloody, gory detail because the film makers had the technology to show it. The remakes of the films take it even further, since contemporary slasher films rely on computer-generated imagery (CGI) for their effects.

These effects add to the shock value, and graphic, gruesome depictions emphasize the killer's inherent evil. The explicit violence in slasher films sets them apart from other horror movies because they emphasize—in full bleeding color—the horrific nature of dying. While many critics, church groups, and family values groups decried such brutality, moviegoing audiences were intrigued.

The fourth basic element of slasher films has to do with setting. The characters are isolated from the rest of society, making a rescue nearly impossible. "Slasher films are notoriously devoid of grown-ups, and the few who are present tend to play three general roles: (1) the killer him or herself; (2) the wise 'seer' or 'elder' who offers advice on how to defeat the killer; or (3) the ineffectual authority figure who refuses to believe or acknowledge the dangers at hand" (Rockoff 11–12). The young characters are forced to rely on their own knowledge to get out of their circumstances alive, which most of them are unable to do. But they are also at another disadvantage.

The setting is often the site where the killer was first traumatized, making him much more familiar with the surroundings than those who are just there visiting. This is especially true in *Psycho*, *The Texas Chain Saw Massacre*, *Halloween*, *Friday the 13th*, *A Nightmare on Elm Street*, and *Scream*. The killer knows where and when to attack because he or she knows where the best hiding places are and how to get from one victim to another undetected. In a sense, the killer has a home field advantage, and that, partnered with the victims' lack of experience, gives the killer the upper hand.

Rockoff's fifth category deals with the past event, the traumatic occurrence that makes the killer kill. This is usually set up as a prologue, taking place years before the rest of the film. It is in this scene that the "killer witnesses a traumatic event, usually to a family member, or is the victim of a devastating, humiliating or harmful accident, prank or tragedy" (Rockoff 12). The killer then feels the need to get revenge and exacts it on the anniversary of the event. Rockoff claims that there are two important reasons for the prologue:

> (1) it grabs the audience's attention and whets their appetite for the carnage that is to come; (2) it gives the audience an explana-

tion for the killer's fury, no matter how unhelpful or ridiculous that explanation may be. . . . [T]his explanation rarely makes the killer a more sympathetic figure, most likely because it is hardly sufficient to explain the level of psychosis these villains display. (13)

The past event reinforces the evil and brutal nature of the killer without allowing the audience to get to know him too well. It may give motive to his actions, but it does not explain the gruesomeness behind them.

The sixth element deals with the Final Girl, the character who is able to vanquish the killer. She is defined from the beginning of the movie as being different from the rest of the group. She is generally tough, smart, strong willed, and perseverant. In most films, she is usually single and not obsessed with sex like her friends. "Much has been made of the masculinity of the Final Girl, which, in the case of the slasher film, is used as a euphemism for strength and compe-tence, not as a reference to sexuality or gender" (Rockoff 13). The Final Girl has the most basic human desire: to survive. Unlike her friends, she is able to do just that because she is focused.

The seventh basic element deals with the subjective point of view. Many slasher films feature scenes from the killer's perspec-tive, a technique that forces the audience to identify with the killer. Because they are allowed to see what the killer sees, they, in effect, become complicit with the murderer: stalking victims with the killer, peering through trees and windows, the audience members become voyeurs. But, the subjective camera can also be used to signify the Final Girl's point of view, allowing the audience to identify with her. This technique, which makes it problematic for the viewer, is used at times to throw the audience off. They may believe that they are looking through the killer's eyes, only to be fooled when he pops out of a hiding place next to them or in the distance. The subjective camera has the ability to make the audience identify with certain characters, but it also creates a sense of anxiety because viewers are never really sure where the gaze is coming from. Subjective camera work is just another technique, like that of gore, to keep the audience on the edge of their seats, wanting more, and it also helps the film's author direct the audience's attention to see exactly what he wants them to see.

One of the most recognized point-of-view scenes comes from *Halloween*. At the beginning of the film, the audience glances into a window with an unseen individual and looks at a girl and boy talking on the couch. He asks if they are alone, and she mentions that Michael is around somewhere. They then head upstairs, and the audience goes with the individual into the house. Through the person's perspective, the audience goes into the kitchen and grabs a butcher knife, then proceeds toward the stairs. On the way up, the unknown individual puts on a clown mask, further limiting the point of view into two peepholes. The individual and the audience head upstairs, where they find the girl sitting at the vanity in her underwear brushing her hair. The audience and assailant approach, stabbing the girl multiple times before running outside. There, they run into an adult and the mask is pulled off the face, ending the first-person perspective and revealing a young boy.

Friday the 13th also uses this technique extensively. In a scene where Annie is attempting to make her way to Camp Crystal Lake, an unseen individual picks her up in a Jeep on the side of the road. The audience watches from the person's perspective as Annie climbs into the vehicle and strikes up a friendly conversation. The Jeep drives down the road and past the turnoff for the camp. When Annie points this out, the driver says nothing and picks up speed. Annie becomes frightened and jumps out of the vehicle. The unknown person comes after her, and the audience watches as the attacker slits Annie's throat with a hunting knife.

In *Friday the 13th*, the use of first-person camera perspective is also used to throw off the audience. In the scene where Marcie is in the bathroom, the camera moves and stares at her as if someone is watching her. She becomes aware that she might not be alone and goes to explore. A sound from the shower draws her attention, and the camera angles make the audience believe the killer is hiding in the stall. When Marcie pulls back the curtain, no one is there. She turns around and the killer slams an ax into her face.

The film that started the slasher genre is up for debate. Some would argue that Alfred Hitchcock's *Psycho* (1960) is actually the first slasher film, and many of the films that fall into the genre pay homage to this masterpiece. This book will focus on *Psycho, Black Christmas, The Texas Chain Saw Massacre, Halloween, Friday the 13th, A Nightmare on Elm Street,* and *Scream* because they had the greatest influence on the slasher genre and have either generated multiple sequels or—with the exception of *Scream*—they have been remade.

Psycho has three sequels and was remade in 1998. *Black Christmas* doesn't have sequels, but it was remade in 2006. *The Texas Chain Saw Massacre* has three sequels and was remade in 2003. Although the original film in the series is not actually considered a slasher, this film is still important because it influenced the slasher genre.

Halloween has eight sequels and a remake that came out in 2007. The *Friday the 13th* films have endured for more than twenty years, with ten sequels, and the remake of this film came out in 2009. *A Nightmare on Elm Street* has seven sequels and was remade in 2010.

There are several reasons why these movies have survived the last few decades and why they have entertained countless audiences.

Rockoff's basic elements of slasher films succinctly summarize the definitions of the genre. They create a clear picture of what is expected in each film. Even though every single film doesn't have to incorporate every single element, or they alter some of the elements, most of them are still present in some form or another. There are a few films that don't follow the formula exactly. As mentioned earlier, *Texas* is one of those, but so is *Scream*. If a film doesn't have these elements, can it still be a slasher?

While the answer can probably be debated, the short answer is yes. Even though *Texas* doesn't give the audience an in-depth look or prologue that explains the traumatic event that turns the killers evil, it is implied that the closing of the slaughterhouse affected them. The Final Girl, Sally, doesn't pick up a weapon and fight against the family, but she doesn't lie down and die, either. She takes the necessary steps to ensure her survival. The film takes place in a secluded area, and the killer uses sharp objects to kill his victims. Even though *Texas* isn't a textbook slasher, it has a few of the required elements.

Scream also functions slightly differently than traditional slasher films. The killer doesn't get a prologue that sets up his traumatic event, and only one of the killers, Billy, was actually traumatized by something. Stuart might have been, but it's never revealed to the audience. The Final Girl, Sidney, fights against and defeats the killers, but she uses a gun to accomplish the task. There aren't any point-of-view shots. It can be argued that the teens aren't isolated from society because the film takes place in the suburbs, but they are. Even though there are adults around, they are inept at protecting the teens. The killers' weapon is a stabbing instrument, and there is a lot of blood to shock the audience.

Slasher films have been torn apart and condemned by critics and many others, but they do have a purpose. They are not only about shock and gore, though that part can't be ignored; they are chockfull of life lessons. The main characters in these films are teens, an in-between group that has to learn how to function in the adult world. The killer acts as the teacher for these skills. The lessons they are attempting to teach include the past catching up with the teens, the need to listen to their elders, and the need to learn from their mistakes. The teens who die are the ones who failed to learn the life lesson.

FILM SYNOPSES

BLACK CHRISTMAS

Year: 1974
Killer: No name
Final Character: Jess
Other Characters: Peter, Barb, Lieutenant Fuller, Mrs. Mac, Phyl, Mr. Harrison, Sergeant Nash, Chris, Clare
Slasher Elements: Killer uses sharp objects to kill victims, including a crystal unicorn or knife; some graphic special effects to shock viewers, such as Mrs. Mac hanging from hook and pulley in attic; sorority house is isolated from rest of society; the killer has been traumatized by death of his sister; Jess picks up a weapon to fight against killer, but winds up killing the wrong man; the killer's point of view is employed.
Basic Plot: Sorority sisters are getting ready to head home for Christmas and are being plagued by mysterious and threatening phone calls. One by one, the remaining girls are murdered by a killer who has taken shelter in the attic. Jess is the last survivor, and the police have discovered the calls are coming from inside the house. Instead of leaving, she wants to make sure her friends are all right, and is attacked by the killer. Her

boyfriend, Peter, discovers her cornered and frightened in the basement and asks if she's okay. Believing he's the killer, she bashes his head in with a fireplace poker. The authorities are convinced the case is solved, completely unaware the real killer is still hiding in the attic.

BLACK CHRISTMAS [REMAKE]

Year: 2006

Killers: Billy and Agnes Lenz

Final Character: Kelli Presley

Other Characters: Melissa, Leigh Colvin, Heather Fitzgerald, Dana, Barbara "Ms. Mac" MacHenry, Lauren Hannon, Kyle Autry, Billy's Mother, Megan Helms, Clair Crosby, Eve Agnew

Slasher Elements: Killers use sharp, penetrating objects to kill sorority sisters, including a fountain pen and crystal unicorn; the weapons stabbing through flesh and eyes being pulled out of sockets are rampant throughout the film; setting is a sorority house isolated from society; Billy was traumatized by his mother who didn't love him and locked him in the attic, Agnes was traumatized when her brother/father tried to kill her; Kelli fights against the killers at the end; points of view from the killer are used.

Basic Plot: Sorority sisters are getting ready to head home for Christmas, while Billy and Agnes are returning to their childhood home. Unable to show love through any other means than death, they kill the girls and prop their corpses around the Christmas tree in the attic.

FRIDAY THE 13TH

Year: 1980

Killer: Mrs. Voorhees

Final Character: Alice Hardy

Other Characters: Marcie Cunningham, Annie, Jack Burrel, Bill, Brenda, Ned Rubinstein, Steve Christy, Enos, the Truck Driver, Sgt. Tierney, Officer Dorf, Crazy Ralph

Slasher Elements: Mrs. Voorhees uses knives or other sharp objects, such as arrows, to kill victims; special effects in the film were the first of their kind and shocked viewers with Jack being stabbed through the neck and Marcie getting an ax in the face; setting is a summer camp isolated from society; Mrs. Voorhees was traumatized into becoming a murderer after her son drowned; Alice picks up a machete at the end of the film and beheads the killer; the audience sees some of the action through the eyes of the killer.

Basic Plot: A group of teens have come to Camp Crystal Lake to make it operational again. Once the camp owner and only adult leaves to go to town, the teens quit working and start having fun. One by one, they are murdered by a vengeful killer. Alice eventually defeats Mrs. Voorhees by beheading her on the shores of Crystal Lake.

FRIDAY THE 13TH [REMAKE]

Year: 2009
Killer: Jason Voorhees
Final Characters: Clay and Whitney Miller
Other Characters: Jenna, Trent DeMarco, Chewie, Wade, Bree, Richie, Lawrence, Nolan, Chelsea, Mike, Amanda, Donnie
Slasher Elements: Jason's weapon of choice is a machete, but he also kills his victims with arrows and antlers on the wall; the machete penetrating a victim's skull and flesh being stabbed are visible to the audience; the teens have gone to their parents' summer home to party, which is isolated from society; the death of Jason's mother traumatized him into becoming a killer; Whitney and Clay fight against Jason at the end; shots from Jason's perspective are used.

Basic Plot: In the beginning, two teens have come to the area around Crystal Lake looking for a marijuana field, convincing their friends they are on a camping trip. Richie, Amanda, and Wade are slaughtered, and Whitney is taken captive by Jason. Six weeks later, another set of teens have come to party in Trent's parents' summer house, while Clay is looking for his sister, Whitney. They each fall victim to Jason until Clay and Whitney are the only ones left.

FRIDAY THE 13TH PART 2

Year: 1981
Killer: Jason Voorhees
Final Character: Ginny Field
Other Characters: Paul Holt, Alice Hardy, Terry, Ted, Crazy Ralph, Sandra Dier, Mark, Jeffrey, Vickie, Scott, Maxwell, Deputy Winslow
Slasher Elements: Jason's weapon of choice is a machete, yet he kills his victims with ice picks and other sharp objects; more graphic effects to shock viewers, such as people being pinned to a bed during intercourse and a machete across the face; again, takes place at an isolated summer camp; Jason was traumatized by his mother's beheading; Ginny picks up a weapon at the end of the film to fight against Jason; audience sees some action and deaths through the eyes of the killer.
Basic Plot: Teens have come to training camp to learn how to be camp counselors. Camp Crystal Lake has now been condemned, but it's close to the training camp. Teens will be teens, and when the opportunity arises, they engage in intercourse and neglect their duties. They are killed by Jason in gruesome fashion.

HALLOWEEN

Year: 1978
Killer: Michael Myers

Final Characters: Laurie Strode and Dr. Sam Loomis
Other Characters: Annie Brackett, Lynda van der Klok, Sheriff
   Brackett, Lindsey Wallace, Tommy Doyle
Slasher Elements: Michael's weapon of choice is a butcher knife; setting is suburban Haddonfield, Illinois, but there are no parents
   around to protect the teens; Michael is traumatized by his sister
   engaging in sex; Laurie fights against Michael and tries to destroy him; view shots are given from killer's perspective.
Basic Plot: On Halloween night when Michael is ten years old, he
   stabs his sister after she has sex with her boyfriend. Afterward,
   he is sent to an asylum. Fifteen years pass, and Michael escapes,
   returning home to kill teens who engage in sexual intercourse.

HALLOWEEN [REMAKE]

Year: 2007
Killer: Michael Myers
Final Characters: Laurie Strode, Annie Brackett, Sheriff Brackett,
   Sam Loomis
Other Characters: Deborah Myers, Ronnie White, Paul, Lynda Van
   Der Klok, Tommy Doyle, Ismael Cruz, Judith Myers, Sheriff
   Brackett
Slasher Elements: Michael kills his victims with a butcher knife;
   stabbing deaths and flesh slicing are seen in detail by the audi-
   ence; setting occurs in suburbs, but the teens are isolated from
   society because no one can protect them from the killer; Michael
   was traumatized by an abusive family and bullies; Laurie fights
   against Michael at end of film; scenes from Michael's perspective are employed.
Basic Plot: At ten years old, Michael has had a hard life. His stepfather was abusive, and he was picked on at school by bullies.
   When he can't take any more of the abuse, he snaps and murders
   his bully, sister, and stepdad. He's sent to an asylum, where he
   spends the majority of his life. When an orderly and his cousin

break in to rape a female inmate, it gives Michael the opportunity to escape and return home. There, he continues his murdering spree and kills teens who engage in sexual intercourse.

A NIGHTMARE ON ELM STREET

Year: 1984
Killer: Freddy Krueger
Final Character: Nancy Thompson
Other Characters: Lt. Donald Thompson, Marge Thompson, Tina Gray, Rod Lane, Glen Lantz
Slasher Elements: Freddy uses knives affixed to a glove to kill his victims; lots of blood and shots of victims being stabbed and cut; victims are attacked in their dreams, which is isolated from society; Freddy was traumatized by parents hunting him down and burning him alive; Nancy fights against Freddy at the end of the film; the killer's perspective is used throughout the film.
Basic Plot: Teens are being attacked and killed in their dreams by an unknown assassin. They eventually discover the man's name is Fred Krueger, and he was a child murderer. When he went free because of a technicality, the parents took justice into their own hands and burned him in a boiler room. He has returned for vengeance and attacks the teens in the one place their parents can't protect them: their dreams.

A NIGHTMARE ON ELM STREET [REMAKE]

Year: 2010
Killer: Freddy Krueger
Final Character: Nancy Holbrook and Quentin Smith
Other Characters: Kris Fowles, Jesse Braun, Dean Russell, Alan Smith, Dr. Gwen Holbrook
Slasher Elements: Freddy affixed knives to a glove to kill his victims; blood and cut flesh are rampant throughout the film; Freddy

attacks the teens in their dreams, which isolates them from society; Freddy was traumatized when the parents sought revenge
for his crimes and burned him alive in a boiler room; Nancy and
Quentin fight against Freddy at the end of the film; points of
view from Freddy's perspective are used.

Basic Plot: Freddy Krueger seeks revenge on the parents who cornered and killed him in a boiler room. He attacks the teens in
the only place the parents can't protect them: their dreams.

PSYCHO

Year: 1960
Killer: Norman Bates
Final Characters: Lila Crane and Sam Loomis
Other Characters: Marion Crane, Detective Arbogast, Sheriff Chambers
Slasher Elements: The killer uses a butcher knife to kill victims;
the Bates Motel is isolated from the rest of society; Norman
was traumatized into becoming a murderer when his mother
found a lover; point of view from killer's perspective is employed.

Basic Plot: Marion steals $40,000 from her boss and heads to Fair-
vale, California, to be with her lover, Sam. Tired and desperate
to get out of the rain, she stops at the Bates Motel, where she
is murdered. Upset by her sister's disappearance, Lila will stop
at nothing until she figures out what has happened to Marion.
This leads to Norman's capture and the revelation that he's had
a psychotic break.

PSYCHO [REMAKE]

Year: 1998
Killer: Norman Bates
Final Characters: Lila Crane and Sam Loomis

Other Characters: Marion Crane, Detective Arbogast, Sheriff Chambers

Slasher Elements: The killer uses a butcher knife to kill victims; the Bates Motel is isolated from the rest of society; Norman was traumatized into becoming a murderer when his mother found a lover; point of view from killer's perspective is employed.

Basic Plot: Marion steals $400,000 from her boss and heads to Fairvale, California, to be with her lover, Sam. Tired and desperate to get out of the rain, she stops at the Bates Motel, where she is murdered. Upset by her sister's disappearance, Lila will stop at nothing until she figures out what has happened to Marion. This leads to Norman's capture and the revelation that he's had a psychotic break.

SCREAM

Year: 1996

Killers: Billy and Stuart

Final Character: Sidney

Other Characters: Casey, Steve, Randy, Mr. Prescott, Gale Weathers, Kenny, Tatum, Deputy Dewey

Slasher Elements: Billy and Stuart use a knife to kill their victims; disemboweling and throat slits are shown in bloody glory; setting is in suburbs, but there aren't many parents around to protect the teens; Billy was traumatized after his mother left because his father had an affair; Sidney fights back against killers at the end.

Basic Plot: A year after her mother's murder, Sidney is ready to move on with her life, but a new set of deaths stirs up the past. Intent on getting revenge for the loss of his mother, Billy kills teens with the help of his friend Stuart. Sidney becomes his main target, because he believes that if he can make her pay, his mother will return.

THE TEXAS CHAIN SAW MASSACRE

Year: 1974

Killer: Leatherface

Final Character: Sally Hardesty

Other Characters: Franklin Hardesty, Jerry, Kirk, Pam, Hitchhiker, Old Man, Grandfather

Slasher Elements: Killer uses knives and sledgehammer to dispatch victims; setting is in rural Texas, far from society; slaughterhouse closed down, traumatizing the family and driving them into insanity.

Basic Plot: Sally and Franklin, along with their friends, are traveling to a cemetery to make sure their family graves have not been disturbed by grave robbers. After ensuring the graves are fine, they pick up a hitchhiker who acts abnormally and scares them. They kick him out of the van and stop to get gas, only to find the local station doesn't have any. While waiting for the gas truck, they head to Sally and Franklin's family home. They stumble onto the Leatherface family, and the teens are murdered until Sally is the only survivor.

THE TEXAS CHAINSAW MASSACRE [REMAKE]

Year: 2003

Killer: Thomas Hewitt (Leatherface)

Final Character: Erin

Other Characters: Morgan, Pepper, Andy, Kemper, Sheriff Hoyt, Jedidiah, Teenage Girl, Old Monty, Luda May, Henrietta, Tea Lady in Trailer

Slasher Elements: Thomas uses a butcher knife and chain saw to kill victims; limbs are cut off, people are stabbed, faces are removed in full glory for the audience to see; the family lives in a small, rural town isolated from the rest of society; Thomas was teased as a child because of a disease that caused parts of his face to fall off; Erin eventually picks up weapons and fights against the Hewitt family; shots from the killer's perspective are used throughout the film.

Basic Plot: On their way home from vacationing in Mexico, Erin and her boyfriend, Kemper, along with their friends, venture through rural Texas. On the way, they pick up a hitchhiker who has obviously been through a traumatic ordeal. While sitting in the backseat of the van, she produces a gun and kills herself. Erin convinces the others to look for help, and they come across the Hewitt family. The teens are slaughtered one by one until Erin is able to escape and make it to safety.

THE PAST WILL CATCH UP WITH YOU

It is easy to look back at the past with a discerning eye and pick and choose the memories that may or may not have actually defined an era. With time and other factors fading the memory and dulling the mind, one can easily look at the past with nostalgia and bemoan the fact that it was better than the present. After all, things were simpler back then. The world wasn't full of so many problems, and teens respected the authority figures.

The killers in slasher films have a tendency to look at the past as the ideal time. Back then, they didn't have to worry about a thing; life was easy and problems were taken care of for them. They chose to forget the bad things, the reality of the past, and create a fictitious history. For example, Norman in *Psycho* wants to return to a time when it was him and his mother, when he was loved and she took care of him. The killer in *Black Christmas* wants to return to a time when his family was intact—same with Mrs. Voorhees and Jason in *Friday the 13th*, along with Michael in *Halloween* and Billy in *Scream*. In *The Texas Chain Saw Massacre*, the family wants to return to the past when they had jobs. In *A Nightmare on Elm Street*, Freddy wants to return to a time when the teens were young and innocent. Their world was perfect.

But then, something happens to change it all, something traumatic. Someone ruined their lives, took the utopia away. In some cases, it was the killer himself, such as the killer in *Black Christmas*, who may or may not have had something to do with his sister's death. Or Michael in *Halloween*, who gets institutionalized after killing his sister. Norman murders his mother and her lover. In some cases, others can be blamed. In *Friday*, irresponsible teenagers let Jason drown. Billy's mother left him after his dad had an affair. Freddy was murdered by vengeful parents. No matter the cause of the tragedy, the killers blame the people around them, mainly teens, and attempt to force their vision of the past onto the present. The teens who refuse to become a part of it are killed.

The focus of slasher films is on how one tragic event transformed an individual into a killer. This event usually traps the killer in the past, even as time progresses, and instills conservative ideals. Any teen or character that does not fit into the killer's idealized past is destroyed.

The Traumatic Event

This event is part of the slasher genre, and every killer experiences it. It defines them and their actions. In some cases, it may be a practical joke that goes horribly wrong. In other instances, a loved one is killed or lost. In either scenario, the killer develops a desire for revenge and sets his gaze on the same type of people who wronged him in the first place. It doesn't have to be the actual people who wronged him; any surrogate who shares the same traits will do.

In *Psycho*, Norman explains to Marion that his dad died when he was five. His mother then met another man who convinced her to build the hotel. They did not get married but instead lived together as lovers. Norman tells her that he, referring to his mother's boyfriend, came to a messy death, but doesn't give details. Later in the film, Lila and Sam find out from the sheriff that supposedly Norman's mother killed her lover and herself with strychnine after she found out he was married to another woman. At the end of the film, the audience is given another story that Norman felt betrayed and abandoned by his mother when she starting seeing the other guy, so he killed them both.

However the deaths of the parental figures occurred in the film, the audience knows that Norman was distressed by the perceived notion that his mother abandoned him. Emotionally, he couldn't get past that feeling and had a psychotic break. He felt so jealous of being replaced by another man, he thought his mother would feel the same way if he had sexual feelings toward another woman. Hence, when Marion sexually arouses him, the jealous mother side comes out and kills her.

There is never a clear indication of what happened to the killer in *Black Christmas* to make him a murderer. The audience gets hints of it during his phone calls, and they can assume that something terrible happened to his sister at a young age. There are indications that he might have been involved with his sister's tragedy and suffered the wrath of his mother. Whatever happened, he felt the need to make the sisters in the sorority pay with their lives.

The traumatic event that occurred to the killers in *The Texas Chain Saw Massacre* is the closing of the slaughterhouse. Technology has replaced human workers, leaving them destitute and without a means to survive. This turns the family into psychotic killers who use their knowledge and ability to kill people who venture into their town. The teens they murder in the film probably didn't have anything to do with the slaughterhouse closing. They are targeted because they are transients without ties and, more than likely, won't be missed by anyone. They are also young and represent chance, which is what traumatized the family in the first place, so they need to be taken care of.

The traumatic event that shaped Michael's life in *Halloween* was his sister's sexual encounter with her boyfriend. Exactly what in that encounter upset him is left to speculation. Did he have an Oedipus complex that was directed toward her? Did he become insanely jealous to see her with another man? Or was he just upset that she didn't take him trick-or-treating? In either case, he becomes upset with any teen that engages or is about to engage in sexual activities.

In the first *Friday the 13th*, Mrs. Voorhees is traumatized by the death of her son. According to her, Jason was a special boy who needed to be watched at all times. He drowned in the lake at summer camp because the counselors were too busy making love instead of watching the children. If she ever punished those teens for not watching her son, the audience never finds out. Instead, she punishes other teens who had nothing to do with her son's death. The only trait they share with the counselors is engaging in premarital sex, and Mrs. Voorhees disciplines them severely for those actions.

Jason's traumatic event occurs when his mother is beheaded on the lakeshore. While it's unclear how he witnessed this since he was supposed to be dead, it becomes the reason for his murderous sprees. Jason actually seeks revenge on Alice for killing his mother, and she becomes the first victim in the second film. However, after that, the other victims are teens who engage in practices that don't agree with Jason's conservative ideals.

In *A Nightmare on Elm Street*, Freddy is traumatized by parents of the neighborhood who take revenge on him for murdering children. He was arrested and tried for his crimes but was able to get off on a technicality. The parents didn't like that, so they trapped him in the boiler room where he took his victims and burned Freddy alive. He desires revenge. Instead of targeting the parents directly, he goes after their children, attacking them in the one place the parents can't protect them.

In *Scream*, Billy is traumatized by his mother's abandonment. His father had an affair with Sidney's mother, and he blames her for breaking up his parents' marriage. He kills Sidney's mother and is able to pin it on someone else, but that isn't good enough. He desires to have his family back, and believes that by torturing and eventually killing Sidney, he'll get it.

It's All Right to Make Up a Past

After the killer has experienced the traumatic event and vowed revenge, he creates a fictitious past and yearns to return to it. He also
adopts conservative ideals, ones that never existed in his past before;
but if they had, everything would have been perfect and he wouldn't
have been transformed into a murderer. Once his past is in place
and his ideals are fixed, he takes it upon himself to discipline those
who don't idolize the fictitious past or practice the same conservative
ideals he does.

Norman creates a past where it is him and his mother. There
are no boyfriends or lovers, just a boy and his mother. He believes
his mother is still alive, and tries to appease her demands, which
includes not viewing women as sexual objects. If they are viewed as
such, they have to be destroyed. He creates an idealized past where
women are nothing more than mothers who desire to take care of
children. Norman wants to be with his mother so bad, he incorporates her personality into his. In his mind, he is still his mother's
boy. He still believes that she will take care of him. He kills Marion
because he views her as a sexual object. He takes on his mother's
personality to kill Marion because she has to protect him, keep him
away from sexual, grown-up desires. But it is exactly those sexual,
grown-up desires that led to his mother's death in the first place.

The focus of *Psycho* is the desire for women to return home and
become wives and mothers. The film opens with Marion and Sam
in a hotel room, obviously after a sexual encounter. They get into an
argument because Marion wants their relationship to be respectable.
She is tired of meeting in hotel rooms and wants Sam to come to
her house for dinner and meet her sister. Her ultimate goal would
be for them to be married, but Sam doesn't have any money, and he
doesn't want her living in a storeroom like he does. There is a vague
promise that one day they will get married, and Marion heads back
to the office. While there, the other secretary tells Marion about her
husband and mother and the relationship between the two when
the boss walks in with a client. The client sits on Marion's desk and

explains to her that he is buying a house for his eighteen-year-old daughter, who is getting married. He sets $40,000 on the desk, and Marion's boss tells her to take it to the bank. Marion seizes the opportunity and steals the money.

Marion is outside of the conservative, fictitious past, and she is killed because she doesn't obey the rules. Aside from being a criminal, she doesn't act like the ideal woman. Even though she desires to get married and be respectable, she has sex outside the bonds of marriage. Ideally, she should have refrained from such an act until she had the ring on her finger. She is constantly reminded of how abnormal she is by everyone around her talking about marriage. When she gets to the Bates Motel and talks to Norman, she realizes the error of her ways and desires to return to Phoenix to make amends. But it's too late; there is no going back. Marion can't return, so she has to die.

Although the desire to return to the past where all women became wives is very strong in this film, it is also impossible. Marion believes she has found the answer to her problems by stealing the money. Perhaps she believes she and Sam will run away to a private island and live happily ever after, but then she begins to have second thoughts when she is fifteen miles from Sam's home. She realizes she was wrong and hopes that if she returns, she will be forgiven. Other characters, such as Sam and Mrs. Bates, represent how the institution of marriage has crumbled. Sam claims that the reason he doesn't have any money is because he has to send it to his ex-wife. He hopes that his ex will eventually get married so he can stop paying her alimony. Mrs. Bates was married at one time, but after the death of her husband, she becomes sexually involved with a man she doesn't wed. Even Caroline's (the other secretary at Marion's work) relationship, which is supposed to be the ideal because she is married, doesn't seem to be the best situation. It appears that her mother is constantly interfering. When Marion asks her if there had been any calls, Caroline tells her that Teddy (Caroline's husband) called, and then her mother called to see if her husband called. Before that, she offers to give Marion some tranquilizers for her headache, which her mother gave her on the night of her wedding. She then explains that her husband was furious when he found out she had tranquilizers. These relationships are not ideal, they are dysfunctional.

Norman desires to return to a conservative past where women were not sexually active, but it is obvious that this past never existed. Norman never had a normal childhood. At the end of the film, the psychiatrist explains that Norman's mother was very clingy and overbearing. For a long time, it was just the two of them, but when the other man entered their life, Norman became jealous, which is why he murdered them. Since Norman didn't know how to live without his mother, he re-created her in his psychosis. He re-created the past. But since it's impossible to return, his actions became destructive on the present. The majority of the relationships in this film are problematic, which explains the desire to return to the ideal, but that can't and won't happen.

The basic premise of *Black Christmas* is the desire to return home. For the sorority girls, this means leaving for the holidays, but for the killer, it is the desire to return to a time before tragedy struck. It's impossible to know for sure because his motives are unclear, but it seems the killer wants to return to a time when his family was intact. The traditional ideal of the home is that it is a safe place to be and is occupied by a mother, father, and 2.5 kids. The sorority house functions as a type of home because it is supposed to be a safe place for the girls, but it does not fit into the ideal because there is only a housemother and no father.

Mrs. Mac is supposed to represent the ideal mother figure. She is the housemother, and her job is to ensure that the girls get a good education and that they remain wholesome. Unfortunately, she is a drunk who cusses and doesn't really care what the girls do. While Mrs. Mac and Mr. Harrison are in Clare's room, looking for a clue of where she might be, he sees the picture of Clare's boyfriend on the dresser. He asks who it is, and Mrs. Mac tells him, making sure to add that he is a nice boy from town. Mr. Harrison reacts with a sour look and tells Mrs. Mac that he did not send his daughter to school to drink and pick up boys and that he is going to do something about it. A little while later, while Mrs. Mac is getting ready to leave, she mocks Mr. Harrison and his threat. Even though she is the housemother, she doesn't feel responsible for making sure all the girls in the house are morally sound. She has enough to worry about, such as finding her hidden bottles of alcohol.

The sorority house also doesn't fit the ideal of home because the women are acquiring an education instead of raising children. It represents the "new home" where women are independent and make choices detrimental to the family. This is especially evident in the relationship between Jess and Peter. She is pregnant, and Peter wants nothing more than to get married and raise a family. Jess wants to fulfill her dreams and desires, and that does not include becoming a mother or a wife. When she tells Peter this, he becomes upset and threatens her. At the end of the film, when Jess is being stalked by the killer, she hides in the basement. Peter happens to find her there, and Jess believes that he is the real killer, so she bashes his head in with a fireplace poker. Peter's death is symbolic of women fighting violently to have lives of their own and not be defined through their husband or children.

The destruction of the home and family threatens to undermine the killer's fictitious past and conservative ideals, so he comes in to reestablish his version of order. The killer in this film is shrouded in mystery. The audience never knows why he is killing the girls in the sorority. There seems to be some indication that he is trying to recover something from his past, something that went terribly wrong. This is evident in the phone calls he makes after committing a murder. There is a sense that he has mixed personalities, and he speaks in several different voices, including one that seems to be his mother or some other female authority figure. Although the audience never knows exactly what happened, they can assume that something happened to his little sister.

The first victim in the film is Clare, who is probably the most innocent of all the girls. She gets upset after the first obscene call, telling Barb she shouldn't provoke people like that. Clare also mentions that a girl from town had been raped recently. Barb sighs and rolls her eyes, telling Clare that "You can't rape a townie." By this point, Clare is angry, so she heads to her room to pack. On her way upstairs, while Jess is telling Barb to be nice because Clare has a hard enough time fitting in, Barb mentions that she knows a professional virgin when she sees one. Clare also doesn't drink as much as the other girls, and she doesn't cuss. Despite this innocence, there are implications that she will not remain that way forever. For example, Clare is the only one in the film who is seen kissing a boy. Her room is decorated with posters that portray an old woman sitting in her rocking chair with an afghan flipping people off and naked people forming a peace sign. She becomes the first target of the killer precisely because of her innocence.

The killer is trying to return to a past where his sister is still alive, and it is assumed that she was young when she died. He kills Clare before she can be influenced by the other sisters or the world of higher education. After her murder, he sets her up in a rocking chair in the attic so she can look out the window. He rocks her back and forth while cooing and even gives her a doll to hold. Even her murder differs from the others. The others are brutally stabbed or impaled, but Clare is suffocated with a bag.

The killer desires to see women in the home instead of getting a college education, and he is not the only one. The sorority sisters are viewed as outsiders by the local townsfolk. This is most evident in how the society in the film refuses to have anything to do with the girls. For example, Barb is on the phone with her mother, making plans to come home for Christmas, but her mother doesn't want her there. Barb's mother is planning on going on a trip with some guy. As Barb asks about the details, she calls her mother a "gold-plated whore." It is further emphasized at the police station when Phyl, Barb, and Mr. Harrison try to report Clare missing. The officer dismisses them and tells them that she is probably "shacked up with some guy." It isn't until Chris, Clare's boyfriend, bursts into the

Clare (Lynne Griffin) stares sightlessly out the attic window in *Black Christmas* (1974). *Warner Bros./Photofest © Warner Bros.*

station and demands that something be done that Lt. Fuller gets involved with the case. The message here seems to be that if you want something done, you need a man to act on your behalf. But having a man act on the women's behalf does not protect them. It doesn't even save them. Chris and the police never find Clare's body. They don't ever find the real killer. He is left in the attic to continue his murdering spree. When Jess needs to be saved, she has to save herself.

The film portrays the desire to return to a time when women stayed in the home, but being in the home is not safe. Presumably, the killer was at home when something happened to his sister. The girls are in a home, albeit a sorority house, but it is still supposed to be a safe place. When a man does enter the house, there are murderous results.

The desire to return to a time and a home when the nuclear family reigned supreme is impossible. The film shows us that the home has been tainted with death, women are thinking for themselves, and men are incapable of keeping them safe.

The family in *The Texas Chain Saw Massacre* desires to return to a time when they had jobs at the slaughterhouse and society hadn't changed, a time when teens respected authority figures, had a work ethic, and were defined by their job. The use of a slaughterhouse motif in the film works on many different levels. On the most obvious level, the audience realizes that the family has substituted people for cows, but the process of killing them is basically the same. On the symbolic level, the slaughterhouse represents the distinction between generations. For Grandpa's generation, killing cows to ensure that the family had food on the table would have been a normal occurrence. More than likely, it would have happened on the ranch instead of in a facility, but it would have happened nonetheless. The transition of Grandpa going from the ranch into the facility would be the transition from an agrarian society into an industrialized one. By shipping livestock to stockyards and butchering them en masse in one facility, it was easy to stock supermarket shelves with meat. The process of killing the cows with a sledgehammer would have been a method similar to that used on the farm, and it got the job done. It wasn't until the younger generation pulled away from the older generation's ideals that this process became monstrous.

Sally's generation, the hippie generation, wanted their world to be different from the world of their parents. For people like Grandpa, cows were seen as food. For people like Sally, cows were viewed as living creatures who had feelings and should die a dignified death. Slaughterhouses came under scrutiny, and the cows had to be killed in a humane manner. It was no longer acceptable to bash them in the head with a hammer; they had to be rendered unconscious before they were killed. Grandpa represents the generation that has been displaced by new ideals.

The slaughterhouse also represents the most base of human desires: to provide families with food. In agrarian societies, the man of the house would teach his trade to his son, and when the father could no longer perform the work, the son would inherit the ranch. In the context of the film, industrialization has upset this balance. It is obvious that the entire Leatherface family has been trained in the slaughter business. When Grandpa worked at the facility, he had a trade to pass on to the next generation. But when his job became obsolete, what did he have for his kids? The Leatherface family is a corrupted version of the nuclear family because industrialization changed societal values. Instead of changing with them, the family passed on the slaughtering tradition; they just turned their focus away from cows and set their sights on people.

The teens (Sally, Jerry, Franklin, Pam, and Kirk) are heading to Sally and Franklin's grandparents' place after hearing on the radio that graves have been desecrated. The teens are obvious representatives of the hippie generation through their dress and fascination with astrology. The teens exist in their own world where nothing is important except for their concerns; they are drifting through space with very few cares in the world. The desire to make sure the family graves have not been disturbed seems to be an excuse to get out on the road. They spend very little time at the cemetery, and where Saturn is in relation to the cosmos and how cows used to be slaughtered make up the bulk of their conversation.

When Sally is captured by the family, the idea of the nuclear family has been convoluted, and she is surrounded by psychotic men. At a crazy dinner where Sally is tied to a chair, the men talk about how Grandpa used to be the best at his job, which was murdering cows at the slaughterhouse with a sledgehammer. When they ask him to kill Sally, he can't even hold the hammer. Grandpa is the embodiment of the idealized past. Legends surround him and how wonderful he was "back in the day," but now he is nothing more than a decrepit corpse that can't carry out the simplest task.

The family desires to return to a time when they and their jobs were more than just work but a means of survival. However, they can't go back. Their surroundings suggest their livelihood is gone. Crops have succumbed to drought, and the cattle that remain are unhealthy and thin. Even if the slaughterhouse reopened, they have no one to pass their skills to. There are no women in the family to have children. The film shows us that the agrarian, rural way of life is tainted with lunacy and death. Industrialization has made it impossible to return to the past.

In *Halloween*, Michael seems to want to return to a time of innocence, and his conservative ideal focuses on teens not being allowed to participate in sexual practices. The victims who are punished in the film are teens who participate or are about to participate in a sexual act. Michael is the avenger who will return the teens to a time of propriety. The first person to die onscreen is Michael's sister, Judith, and she is killed right after having sex with her boyfriend. "Linda and Danny are killed in the postcoital moment. . . . Annie is killed before she has engaged in an onscreen sexual act, but she is preparing to engage in illicit sexual behavior."[1] Even thinking about having sex in this film is cause enough for murder.

This past Michael wants to return to is fictitious and never existed. He was ten when he murdered his sister, killing any type of innocence that would have existed within him. After that, he spent fifteen years in an asylum. When he breaks out and returns home, the place has been abandoned, and his parents are gone. He can't return to an ideal that only existed in his mind.

Both Jason and Mrs. Voorhees desire to return to a time when their family was intact. Since Jason drowned because the counselors were busy making love, Mrs. Voorhees focuses her revenge on kids who engage in premarital sex or come back to the camp to be a counselor. Jason focuses his murderous rage on anyone who ventures into or close to Camp Crystal Lake. His mother was beheaded by an outsider, so every other outsider must pay. Like his mother, he also targets teens who engage in premarital sex or experiment with drugs.

For Jason and his mother, the past would have been ideal if teens weren't engaging in risky behaviors. They desperately want to return to this pristine era, but it never existed. The most glaring example of this can be seen in the character of Jason, who supposedly drowned when he was a child, and then was found living in a shack in the woods. Jason first makes his appearance in the second *Friday* movie. How and why he has survived in the woods is never explained, and his only real contact with society would have occurred when he was a kid, and he had to obey the authority figures then. His perceptions of the past revolve around the fact that everything he needed was provided to him by his mother; he never had a chance to grow up and learn how to become independent. His desire is to return to a time when his mother was still alive and took care of things for him. But she has been killed.

Mrs. Voorhees and Jason desire to return to the ideals of the fifties. In their fictitious past, that was an era that focused on the nuclear family and only worried about threats coming from distant places outside society. Jason drowned at summer camp, not because alien invaders came down and attacked the place, but because members of society were irresponsible, which would place Mrs. Voorhees in a position where she is unable to trust the teens within the culture. The tragedy occurred back in 1957, when the stereotype was that teens weren't having premarital sex. Obviously, this is an incorrect assumption because Jason drowned while the counselors were making love, and the opening sequence of *Friday the 13th* shows two teens going off to find a private area in the barn. Mrs. Voorhees corrects the teens' behavior through murder, which would make it difficult for the lesson to sink in.

Mrs. Voorhees explains her motives to Alice, but never once does she mention anything about Jason's father, which is problematic if the ideal of the past stresses that two parents need to be present to raise a child. We know that she was married—she is a Mrs.—but it is not until we get to *Jason Goes to Hell* that an explanation of what happened to the father is offered. We know from this film that Diana and Jessica share the same bloodline as Jason, but Mrs. Voorhees claims that she only had one son, so Diana would be the product of Jason's father and another woman. Now, the exact details of Jason's father and what he may or may not have done is left to a lot of speculation; my only point here is that when he was supposed to be present, he wasn't. Perhaps if Mrs. Voorhees had him as a support system, she wouldn't have turned into a vengeful murderer.

The other aspect of Mrs. Voorhees that makes her idealized past completely fictitious is that, like her son, she was never part of the film's society. In the movie, the first murders at Camp Crystal Lake took place in 1958, and the attempt to reopen the camp, when teens are once again present, takes place in 1980. The townsfolk speak about Jason drowning, but they never mention anything about what happened to his mother; she just seems to have disappeared from this small town for twenty-two years. One would tend to think that after all this time, she would have been able to get over the death of her son and move on, but the fact that she hasn't is what makes her so destructive. The lessons Jason and his mother are trying to teach the teens are from a culture that only existed within their minds.

Like Sally's grandparents' house in *Texas*, the summer camp in *Friday the 13th* is supposed to be a place full of fond childhood memories. But like Sally's house, the camp is falling apart and tainted with death. The earlier attempts to reopen the camp were thwarted by Mrs. Voorhees lighting fires and poisoning the water. Any good memory of the place was eradicated by Mrs. Voorhees after the death of her son.

The new group of counselors have come to the camp to try and put those bad memories out of their mind. Since they weren't part of Mrs. Voorhees's fictitious past, they want nothing to do with it. People warn them to stay away, but they don't listen. When Steve, the camp's owner and only adult present at the camp, is around, the teens dutifully work at getting the camp ready for the kids. As soon as he leaves, the teens begin having sex and playing strip Monopoly. This is also when they begin dying.

By casting a middle-aged woman as the killer, the director hoped to throw the audience off guard, and for all intents and purposes, he was successful. When looking at it from an idealized past perspective, a woman is an ideal choice. If the focus was to return to a time when the nuclear family reigned supreme, then the woman was an integral part, especially as a wife and mother. The audience never knows what happened to Mr. Voorhees, he is just absent; and when Mrs. Voorhees loses her son, she has completely lost her family. Her desire to return to a time when the family was complete is so strong that she has incorporated her son's personality into her own. As she hunts Alice down, she speaks to herself in a high-pitched, childlike voice. Mrs. Voorhees so desperately wants her family back, she experiences a psychotic break.

In order for Alice to break away from Mrs. Voorhees's desire to return to the past, she has to physically separate herself from the person and the camp. She accomplishes this by beheading Mrs. Voorhees and then by drifting in a boat on Crystal Lake. She is so exhausted from her ordeal that she passes out and wakes up in the morning to see sheriff's officers on the bank. Feeling confident that she is safe, she smiles and drapes her fingers in the water, then is attacked by a deformed boy who grabs her and pulls her off the boat. The next scene shows Alice in a hospital bed, wondering what happened to the boy. The deputy tells her that they didn't find any boy, but she is convinced Jason came back and attacked her. The lesson: no matter how hard you try to forget or get away from the past, it always has a way of coming back and grabbing you.

Freddy wants to return to a time when he could kill children without fear of repercussions from angry parents or the law. *Nightmare* functions differently than other slasher films because the teens aren't being killed because of what other teens did in the past, they are being killed for what their parents did. The killer is attempting to return to an idealized past, and the desire in the film is to return to innocence.

The nuclear family has disintegrated, and no one is trying to rebuild it. Tina's father abandoned her ten years ago, and her mother runs off to Vegas with her boyfriend. Nancy's parents are divorced and barely keep their anger in check when they are around each other. In the context of the film, it seems to be the fault of the fathers for the family falling apart. They either abandon them (Tina) or use them for their own ends (i.e., Nancy's father uses her as bait to capture Rod after Tina's murder). The one father who is present in the family (Glen's) dooms his son to death when he takes the phone off the hook so Nancy can't wake him.

With fathers largely absent from the family picture, it is up to the mothers to ensure their children's safety, and they aren't doing such a wonderful job. Tina's mom is there when she wakes screaming from a nightmare, asking if everything is all right and telling her she needs to cut her nails after she discovers Tina's nightgown is ripped, but then she leaves Tina alone to go to Vegas with her boyfriend. Marge is always there to make sure Nancy doesn't drown in the bathtub or to turn off the TV when the newscast talks about the murder of her friend. She gets Nancy help when the nightmares become so bad that Nancy refuses to sleep. Yet she is the whole reason that Nancy is being stalked by Freddy. Not only did she burn him in the building he killed his victims in, she took his knife glove.

None of the parents told the children about Freddy or what they did to him, even when he stalks them in their dreams. They believe that if they keep the information from the children, they cannot be harmed. The parents desire to keep their kids innocent, and that means protecting them from unpleasant things. The best example of this is when Marge puts the bars on the door and windows of their house. Even though Nancy has told her repeatedly that she is being attacked in her dreams, Marge still believes the threat is coming from the real world. There is no way Marge can protect her daughter in her dreams, so she does something in the real world so she doesn't feel helpless.

Unfortunately, parents can't protect their children all the time, and as they get older, the kids don't really want them to. The teens in the film are right on the border of wanting to do things on their own and still needing their parents around. Tina is freaked out about the nightmare she has, but she doesn't divulge that information to her mother. When her mother leaves to go to Vegas, Tina wants

Nancy and Glen to stay the night at her house so she is safe. Tina is innocent enough that she is frightened by a dream, yet old enough to be having sex. She becomes the first victim because of her inability to return to the innocence of childhood. The same scenario goes for Rod.

Glen is a slightly different case because he doesn't actually engage in sexual activity, although he would if he could. His innocence is more intact than Tina's or Rod's, but he still tries to get Nancy to make out with him and stays up late to watch *Miss Nude America*.

The teens have no desire to return to the past; they are content getting older. Freddy desires revenge on the parents, but he also derives pleasure from killing the teens. After all, he was a child murderer. Freddy wants to return to a time of innocence, but he can't. The kids are growing up. Plus, he's dead and can only attack in nightmares.

As is the case with most slasher films, the desire in *Scream* is to return to a time when the nuclear family reigned supreme. This is especially true for Billy, whose family was destroyed by an extramarital affair. The focus of the film is on Sidney and her attempt to get over her mom's brutal murder, which happened the year before. Things finally seem to be getting back to normal when murders start happening again. Sidney finds the media attention and police presence too much to handle because it reminds her of that fateful day. The killer, who turns out to be Sidney's boyfriend, Billy, purposely orchestrates his murders to coincide with this anniversary because his mother left his father after he had an affair with Sidney's mom. In his mind, if he can make both of them pay for what they've done, his mother will return and they will live as a happy family.

Sidney wants to believe that her mother didn't engage in extramarital affairs and that she was prudish and not sexually active, as the rumors report her to be, but as the film progresses, she learns that her mother may have been as promiscuous as everyone claims. This promiscuity is punished because it threatens the institution of the family.

There are indications in the film that Sidney may have been like her mother. When Billy climbs into her bedroom from the window, he claims that they used to be hot and heavy, but now she could barely stand to be touched by him. Sidney explains that she is trying to get over that, and makes a comment later in the film, after she and Billy have sex, that the reason she never engaged in such activity was because she didn't want to turn out like her mother. Most teens in slasher films try to distance themselves from the previous generation by acting outside of accepted societal norms. In earlier films, this meant engaging in sexual activity and using drugs, because the idealized past would have shunned those behaviors. In later films, if the next generation wanted to act differently than their parents, that would mean *not* engaging in sexual activity or using drugs. This ties into the idea that the teens from previous films are now adults, who have already broke the rules and engaged in antisocial behaviors. But, as the film points out, that doesn't happen. Sidney was able to fight her desires for a while, but she still gave in to them in the end.

It is interesting to note that within *Scream*, the Final Girl is the only one the audience actually sees engaging in any type of sexual activity. While it is implied her friends may be doing the same, we never see it. She is also not the only survivor; she has help from other characters in the film to defeat the killers. This is not a new convention. Several earlier slasher films played with different survivors at the end, including having Final Boys (several of the later *Friday* films played with this convention, and in *Psycho*, both Sam and Lila survive).

Scream takes the conventions of its predecessors and tries to turn them on their heads. While the teens in earlier films were unaware of the dangers that surround them, the teens in *Scream* build on knowledge learned from watching earlier movies. The film constantly refers to the movies from the '70s and '80s. It even pays homage to them through visual cues (a janitor at the high school dressed like Freddy), by mentioning the names of previous films (e.g., *Friday the 13th*, *Terror Train*, *Prom Night*), to actually having

Halloween playing on the TV at a party. The teens know what they have to do to survive, but, unfortunately, this does not save them.

Scream even adds two killers to the film to keep things interesting, and it makes the killers teens instead of an adult from the previous generation. The addition of the second killer doesn't change the convention. When Sidney asks Stuart why he is killing, he claims that it was because of peer pressure. Although he doesn't seem to have a desire to return to the past like Billy, that doesn't mean he doesn't have a motive. What that motive is, the audience never knows. Despite all these changes, the premise remains the same: the killer wants to return to an ideal past and tries to force the teens to do the same. The Final Girl still fights violently against the return and overcomes the killer.

Women Should Know Their Place

If these films are supposed to be a return to an idealized past, then it would stand to reason that women are a central theme because they act outside of normal social boundaries. It can be argued that slasher films portray antifeminist sentiments through the use of an extremely masculine killer and by the type of women who get killed. This is especially evident in *Black Christmas*. The majority of the characters killed are women. In fact, only one man is killed in the film—a cop—and the audience doesn't even see the killer murder him. The women have gone against societal norms and are getting an education and living together in a sorority house. They drink, cuss, hang offensive posters in their room, and have premarital sex. The Final Girl in the film is pregnant and planning on having an abortion, much to the dismay of her boyfriend and, more than likely, the killer. Even though the audience doesn't see it onscreen, it is implied that Jess is murdered just like her sisters. In the views of society, the smart, independent female has to be killed so that other women can see what the consequences are for going against social norms.

In *The Texas Chain Saw Massacre*, the teens represent the hippie generation, which was very influential in reviving and enacting many changes in the women's movement. In *Halloween*, the girls who have or are about to engage in sexual activity are killed. Same case in *Friday the 13th*. In the majority of these films, the Final Girl is the girl who does not engage in sexual activity and has the values and morals that most closely match the ideal woman from the 1950s.

Most killers in slasher films are male and extremely masculine. Their murderous acts toward women can be looked at as punishment for not returning to the roles they are supposed to fulfill. The use of first-person camera work in slasher films represents the oppressive, powerful discourse and is usually set up to be from a male perspective. One of the main acts that the killers perform in slasher films is a voyeuristic stalking of their victims. He watches from behind a bush or a window as they undress or prepare to engage in sexual activity. Normally, the teens who are the subject of the gaze are unaware they are even being watched. The killer is in a position of power while the teens are helpless and become victims. But as the killer watches them, so does the audience. This technique comes under criticism because the subject of the gaze is normally a half-naked woman and the majority of the audience is supposedly male. Some[2] argue that this further objectifies female characters because the male members of the audience identify with the killer and share his vision as he murders his victims.

The Final Girl is able to survive because she shares the power of the gaze. She becomes aware that someone is in the bush or outside the window, and, even though she might not see him, she is able to stare back. By the end of the film, since she has the power of the gaze, she is able to defeat the killer. When the power shifts to her, the audience goes with her. The male members of the audience are then able to identify with her and relish in the revenge she enacts on the killer.

First-person camera work is used in many slasher films, but to view it as an antifeminist construction is problematic. In some cases, the technique is used to throw the audience off. They may believe that they are looking through the killer's perspective, but then the killer steps out from another place onscreen. In some cases, it is not only the killer and Final Girl who have the power of vision, but other characters as well. For example, almost every character in *Psycho* has first-person vision. Marion has it several times in the film, from looking through the windshield when she sees her boss on the crosswalk to looking in the rearview mirror at the cop. Detective Arbogast has it when he enters the Bateses' home while looking for Mrs. Bates. Clare in *Black Christmas* knows that someone is in her closet, and while she is looking, trying to figure out who it is, the audience sees from her perspective for a moment. Although she temporarily has the power of the gaze, it does not save her from being killed. When Tina is dreaming in *A Nightmare on Elm Street*, the audience is subjected to her gaze, albeit temporarily. In *Scream*, they take the notion of first-person camera to a different level. While trying to get the story about the murders, Gale Weathers places a camera in the house the kids are partying at. She and her cameraman sit in the van and watch as the carnage unfolds. They become voyeurs to what is going on inside. They see what is going on, they see the killer attack, but since there is a thirty-second delay, they can't do anything to save the teens. In a way, they become the representations of the audience because all they can do is watch but not act.

The claim of the killer in slasher films being extremely masculine is problematic also. In most slasher films, the killers are portrayed as being masculine, large, and muscular, but despite their manly physical characteristics, they have female traits as well (see lesson 3 for a more in-depth discussion on this subject), exhibit childlike tendencies, or are women. The killers normally kill men and women alike, making it difficult/problematic to claim that they are targeting women just because they are women.

Antifeminist sentiments are further discredited by the act of the Final Girl defeating the killer. If the desire is to return to an ideal past where women knew their place, then the Final Girl should not pick up a weapon and defend herself. After all, she is the representation of the ideal: she is a virgin, she is motherly, she obeys the rules. These Final Girls exist in *Texas*, *Halloween*, *Friday the 13th*, and *A Nightmare on Elm Street*. By having this particular girl become the only survivor, it reinforces how the past the killer wants to return to no longer exists. But even having a Final Girl who doesn't fit into the ideals still reinforces the fictitious past. The Final Girls in *Black Christmas*, *Friday the 13th Part 2*, and *Scream* are not virgins, yet they can still overcome the killer.

If these films were truly antifeminist, why have men die at all? Why have the Final Girl be the only one who actually tries to follow the conventions of society? The point of these films is the desire to return to the past, and, yes, that means that women are supposed to return to their place in the home. But these films also emphasize that the past cannot be returned to, and those that have to fight the hardest against that return are women. They do not portray antifeminist sentiments but instead show just how strong women are and what they have to overcome to function in society.

How to Survive

Most of the characters in slasher films don't survive. For the vast majority of them, it is because they act outside the killer's conservative ideals and notions of the past. The Final Characters usually survive because they portray some of the qualities the killer finds admirable.

Lila is able to survive her encounter with Norman Bates because she is the opposite of her sister. If Marion is supposed to represent what is wrong with women (engaging in premarital sex and stealing), then Lila should be the ideal because she doesn't do either of those things. However, she is not exactly the stereotype of the woman society is looking for. Lila may not engage in premarital sexual activity, but she isn't docile, either. She is loud and demanding and refuses to believe what the men tell her about her sister. She is constantly pushing Sam further to find out where Marion is. When she doesn't get the answers she wants, she goes out and finds them herself.

Lila is not a traditional Final Girl because she doesn't pick up a weapon and fight against the killer. Like other Final Girls, she knows that something is going on at the Bates Motel and she will not rest until she finds out what it is. Just because she doesn't defeat the killer and has to be saved by Sam, she still exposes Norman for the psychopath he is. If it wasn't for her prying, the men in the film would have been content believing Marion ran off with the detective.

The end of *Black Christmas* is problematic. There is never a resolution with the killer. Although she is not a typical Final Girl, Jess displays many of the traits typical of the character. She is the last survivor, she finds the majority of her friends' bodies after they have been killed, and she picks up a stabbing instrument to fight back. However, there is no indication that she actually survives the ordeal. The implication at the end of the film is that Jess dies. The characters in the film figure out that the killer makes his obscene calls after he murders a victim. As the credits roll, the phone rings inside the house. It can be assumed that while all the men are out taking care of other things, Jess was left unattended, and the killer crawled down from the attic and disposed of her. However, since the audience doesn't actually see this happen, they can make up their own minds about what happened to Jess.

Sally in *The Texas Chain Saw Massacre* shares some of the same traits as the Leatherface family because she has moments of idealizing the past and she believes family is important. After stopping at the cemetery to make sure the graves are all right, the teens stop at a gas station to fill up, only to find there is no gas. Sally and Franklin's family house is just up the road, so they decide to wait there until the tanker truck shows up. While there, Sally takes her friends back to the past by taking them on a tour of the home and explaining all the things she used to do as a child. Sally points at the wallpaper, which is barely visible under layers of dirt on the sections that haven't peeled off the wall, and talks about how she used to have a thing for zebras. At first, it seems like fanciful recollections of innocent childhood memories, but then she explains that the only time she was really there was when she was eight, after her grandma died. This return to the past plays into the idea that nothing is what it seems and memories from the past are idealized subjectively. Sally is remembering fond childhood memories of spending time in the house, but the actual circumstances of why she was there are anything but fond.

Sally and Franklin's relationship is pretty close to a normal sibling connection. They argue about who had the knife last in the van, and Franklin gets upset when everyone is upstairs laughing. He mocks their laughter and blows raspberries at the ceiling. Like normal siblings, Sally ignores her brother when he is trying to tell her a story, and feigns interest when he won't leave her alone. But underneath all this normal sibling behavior, there is a sense of duty because of his handicap. This is most evident in the scene when they are waiting for everyone to come back to the van. It is extremely obvious that Franklin is afraid of the dark and doesn't want to be left alone. Sally wants to find her boyfriend. Despite the obvious limitations of pushing a wheelchair through rocks and trees, Sally takes him with her so he doesn't have to be alone. This, of course, leads to Franklin's death and Sally's capture.

Unlike the family, she doesn't go out of her way to protect her brother. When Leatherface jumps out of the bushes and kills Franklin, Sally screams and runs away. She has no desire or concern to make sure he's all right, just a need to survive. The family catches her and hold her captive in their house, which is like a time capsule. Relics from the past, such as the bones of previous victims, litter the floors. Even Grandma still sits in her chair. Sally becomes trapped in their fictitious past.

In order for Sally to escape, she has to physically break free from the clutches of the past, which is symbolized by her crashing through a second-story window. As one would expect, she is hurt in the process, both mentally and physically. She has been affected by the family's idealized past, and she will always take that memory with her. But unlike the family, Sally is able to move forward; she is not stuck in a static state. If you imagine the road as a timeline, Sally moves forward while in the truck, while Leatherface is stuck in one spot, angrily revving his chain saw and spinning in a circle. It is obvious by the end of the film that Sally has no desire to return to the house, just like no one, including the family, is able to return to the idealized past.

In *Halloween*, Laurie is able to survive her encounter with Michael because she does not engage in any sexual practices like her friends. She thinks about boys, but she is too much of a bookworm and "Girl Scout" to even go on a date with them. But that doesn't protect her from being stalked or wounded by the killer. In order for her to break free from Michael's desire to return to the past, she must fight violently against him. While Sally had to physically break through a window in *Texas* to escape, Laurie has to push Michael through a window in order to break free of his influence. Even though she put up a good fight, she still needs the assistance of Dr. Loomis to help fend off Michael, and even then, he is not dead. As Dr. Loomis glances out the window while comforting Laurie, he notices that Michael has vanished.

Like Laurie, Alice in *Friday the 13th* is able to survive because she doesn't engage in sexual practices like her friends. Even though she plays strip Monopoly, she doesn't lose any of her clothes. Like Laurie, she senses that something is amiss and goes to investigate. When she finds the bodies of her friends, she knows she is in a survival situation. Of course, when she first meets Mrs. Voorhees, Alice doesn't realize she is the killer. She throws herself into Mrs. Voorhees's arms and hopes they can find help together. It isn't until Mrs. Voorhees attempts to kill her that Alice realizes she must fight back. Alice defeats Mrs. Voorhees on the banks of Crystal Lake after the two fight. Alice uses the machete to chop off the older woman's head.

Nancy survives in *A Nightmare on Elm Street* because she is the most innocent. She cares about her friends and making sure they are safe instead of her own desires, which is why she turns Glen down at Tina's house. Like Tina, she has moments when she needs her parents to protect her and moments when she wants to protect herself. This is most evident in the bathtub scene. Nancy is drifting to sleep in the tub, and her mom is on the other side of the door, warning her to be careful so she doesn't drown. Marge tells her that she has a glass of warm milk to help her fall asleep, and Nancy replies with a childish, "Warm milk. Gross." Despite her mother's warning, she falls asleep in the tub and is pulled underwater by Freddy. During the struggle, she screams for her mom to save her. She eventually pulls herself out, and when Marge bursts into the bathroom, Nancy tells her that she must have misheard her and that she just slipped getting out of the tub.

Other examples of how Nancy is in between needing to be saved and saving herself include the sleep institute and the final fight with Freddy. Although she isn't too excited about going to the sleep institute and being hooked up to a machine, she does it because her mother asks her to. She realizes that the only way her mom is going to believe her about Freddy is if she can prove his existence, which she does by bringing his hat into the real world from the dream world. After Glen's murder, she needs someone to bash Freddy when she brings him into the real world. Since her dad is across the street, she calls and asks him to come to the house in twenty minutes so he can save her. When he doesn't show up and she wakes herself, she screams for him out the window, but he still doesn't show up until she has defeated Freddy herself.

Despite moments of needing her parents to be there for her, which they rarely are, she also realizes that she has to take steps to protect herself. She reads books about survival and booby-traps the house. The realization that she has to defeat Freddy herself comes after her mother explains how they killed him. At that moment, roles are reversed. Marge can no longer protect Nancy, and that is symbolized in the scene where Nancy puts her mother to bed. This is also why Freddy is able to kill Marge; she reverts to a childlike stage, but she can never return to innocence.

Although Nancy realizes she has to protect herself and that adults cannot help her, her innocence still makes her believe that if she just turns her back on Freddy, takes away the power she supposedly gave him, that will be enough to defeat him, and the film makes the audience believe that this is true. Freddy vanishes right as he lunges for her.

The end of the film has a happy quality to it. Nancy is reunited with her mother, and her friends pull up in a convertible to pick her up. But there is also a surreal quality to it. The world is misty, and Marge explains it is fog that is supposed to clear up later. When Nancy enters the vehicle, the top, which is colored like Freddy's sweater, slams down and the window roll up, trapping the kids inside. The car then drives off down the road, with Nancy pounding and screaming on the window, while Marge waves obliviously from the porch. When the car is out of view, Freddy pulls Marge through the window.

Nancy's childlike beliefs make her believe that she can defeat Freddy by wishing him out of existence. Unfortunately, this didn't happen. The adult world is treacherous and full of danger, and those things don't go away because Nancy wants them to. The only thing that is going to prepare her for coping with the world is guidance from her parents, but they aren't teaching her what she needs to know. She comes to this realization at the end, but by then, it's too late.

Sidney's stand at the end against the killers is the same stand other Final Girls had to face in previous films. Billy wants to return to a time when his family was whole and happy, but that is impossible. While it's possible Sidney would also like to have a family that is whole and complete, she realizes that her notions of the past have been false and tainted by her own perceptions. This is evident when she and Tatum sit on Tatum's porch. Sidney questions whether what she saw the night of the murder was actually true, and wonders what her mother was doing. Tatum points out that Sidney's mother might have been really unhappy since her husband was always traveling, and probably did find comfort in other men's arms. Sidney tries to fight that notion at first but then realizes it may be the truth. Her ability to let the idealized past go is what saves her in the end. Like killers from previous films, it is Billy's one-track mind and inability to see that a return to a fictitious past is impossible that leads to his ultimate defeat.

Conclusion

If these films have shown us anything, it is that the desire to return to the past can result in a very violent encounter. The killers represent the ideals that never existed or have been corrupted, but they are adamant about returning. The majority of the teens in the films die because they are breaking some rule or virtue, and the killers believe it is their duty to punish them. But it can be argued that the reason the teens die is because they are denied a future. If they won't join the killers in a return to the past, then they cannot live to create a different future. Only the Final Girl, who possesses some of the traits the killers find virtuous, is able to defeat the killer and guarantee herself a future, but she doesn't come out of the ordeal unharmed or unchanged by the encounter.

Notes

1. Kendall R. Phillips, "*The Exorcist* (1973) and *The Texas Chainsaw Massacre* (1974)," in *Projected Fears: Horror Films and American Culture* (Westport, Conn.: Praeger, 2005), 137.

2. See Vera Dika, *Games of Terror:* Halloween, Friday the 13th, *and the Films of the Stalker Cycle.* (London: Associated University Presses, 1990).

LISTEN TO YOUR ELDERS

The lessons society teaches are that children must progress into teens, and from teens they must acquire the skills they need to function as adults, and then they must become independent from their parents. They are supposed to learn from the authority figures and not question anything.

The killers in slasher films step in as surrogate authority figures. In most slasher films, parents are absent or ineffectual at their jobs. The killer feels responsible to pass on what the parents can't or won't. However, the lessons they are teaching come from the killer's idealized fictitious past and conservative ideals that were created after they were traumatized. Therefore, the lessons the killers are passing down have no application in the teens' world and are incredibly destructive.

The function of slasher films is to show how the killers in the film function like demons, who have historically been used in fairy tales and stories as an instructive device to teach children the proper ways to act within a culture, which is done through the use of allegory. The function of allegory is to say one thing but mean something different. The author may choose to have their allegory hidden within a text or right there on the surface. There are several different types of allegory, but one of the most important is the notion of the demonic.

> Daemons, as I shall define them, share this major characteristic of allegorical agents, the fact that they compartmentalize function. If we were to meet an allegorical character in real life, we would say of him that he was obsessed with only one idea, or that he had an absolutely one-track mind, or that his life was patterned according to absolutely rigid habits from which he never allowed himself to vary. It would seem that he was driven by some hidden, private force; or, viewing him from another angle, it would appear that he did not control his own destiny, but appeared to be controlled by some foreign force, something outside the sphere of his own ego.[1]

This definition helps us to understand how the role of the killer is defined within the film and how he is perceived culturally. Their inability to vary their habits classifies these killers as demons in the ritual world who are obsessive and try to control every aspect of their world, including the teens, and they act within a completely repetitive system. These killers can be viewed as the representatives of a society that is repressive, obsessive, repetitive, and driven by conservative ideals.

Beware of the Bogeyman

One of the most common uses of demonic allegory is bogeymen. Traditionally, bogeymen do not have a specific set of characteristics; they are generic creatures created to keep children from being naughty. Bogeymen are social constructs that target specific undesirable traits and try to correct them. The killers in slasher films function as a type of bogeyman, and they punish the teens when they overstep the cultural rules. In *Psycho*, *Texas*, and *Friday the 13th*, the teens have to travel outside of society to find the bogey, but in *Black Christmas*, *Halloween*, *A Nightmare on Elm Street*, and *Scream*, the bogeyman finds them.

The main purpose of the bogeyman is to be present and punish when the parents are not around. In essence, they take on the role of the authority figure and impose rules and order. Although in these films it might not seem like it, the killers are trying to enforce some social boundaries, even if that boundary is of their own construction. For example, in *Psycho*, Marion acts outside of accepted sexual norms. She is punished because of her desire and the desire she invokes in others. She is also outside of accepted social norms because she steals money, but she is not punished for that. The client she stole the money from is upset, but instead of calling the police, he hires a private detective to find her. He implies earlier in the film that the reason he has so much money is because he doesn't claim all of it on his taxes, placing him outside of normal social boundaries as well. Plus, while talking to Norman, Marion realizes taking the money was wrong and decides to go back to Phoenix to makes amends, but never once does she think having premarital sex is wrong. Norman's action against Marion is not fueled by money but his desire for her.

Norman functions as the bogeyman and punishes Marion for her deeds because no one else can. A police officer finds her sleeping in her car on the side of the road and asks what she is doing. Of course, she is nervous because she just stole a bunch of money. The cop realizes she is acting peculiar, but since he has nothing to charge her with, he lets her go. When she stops at the used car lot to buy a new car, the cop sees her again and pulls over on the side of the road to watch her. When she leaves, he approaches the dealer and questions him about the transaction. Again, he only has suspicion and nothing concrete to go after her with. Plus, having sex is not illegal, just frowned upon outside the context of marriage. As the authority figure, the cop has to function within the rules and boundaries of society. But Norman as a bogeyman is outside the rules and boundaries and can punish Marion any way he sees fit.

The girls in *Black Christmas* drink, swear, have sex, and are independent thinkers. They threaten the sanctity of the home, so they

Marion (Janet Leigh) cautiously looks for her license and registration in Alfred Hitch-cock's Psycho. Paramount Pictures/Photofest © Paramount Pictures

have to be destroyed. The killer in this film makes a good bogeyman because the audience never sees what he looks like. He is generic. He hides in the attic and only comes down to enact his punishment on the girls. Like *Psycho*, there are police who portray the authority figures in this film, and like the cop in *Psycho*, they are powerless to actually do anything against the killer. They can't even save Jess. Since they have to operate in the world of facts and evidence, when their main suspect, Peter, ends up dead, they are ready to close the case. Again, since the killer operates outside of these boundaries, he is free to continue his murdering spree.

The teens in *Texas* are traveling free across the countryside without a care in the world. They don't have jobs, and they stumble across a family that has lost its only source of income. The teens are stuck at Sally and Franklin's family home because the local gas station is out of gas. While waiting, Pam and Kirk decide to go swimming, only to find the water hole has dried up. They wander into the neighbor's yard, drawn by the sound of a generator, and go to the house in the hopes they can barter for some gas. What they are planning on bartering is unclear since they don't have anything. They are killed in the process. The conservative ideal of the past was that you worked for everything you owned. The hippie generation believed everyone should share with each other. As the bogeyman, the Leatherface family is there to show the teens they cannot freeload off those who have worked hard. This is most evident when they pick up Hitchhiker. While trying to make a buck and survive, he takes a picture of Franklin and offers to sell it to him for five dollars. When Franklin refuses, he burns it ritualistically in the van. The teens don't understand why he would do this and probably believe he should have just given them the picture since he already took it. Hitchhiker doesn't believe in giving something for nothing, so he gets rid of the material possession. The same can be said about the teens as working individuals. Since they are not contributing to society in a productive capacity, the family finds another way to make them useful—as food.

The Leatherface family also serves as a reminder of how dangerous it is to talk to strangers. All kids are taught to be wary of strangers and to never get in a car or let someone in their car they don't know. This is especially important when dealing with people outside the normal social boundaries. The hippie generation wanted to believe everyone was full of goodness and was willing to help out a fellow man. As indicated in the film, this type of thinking was very dangerous and could get you killed. Again, the first instance of this is when the teens pick up Hitchhiker. They believe they are doing a good deed, but that act comes back to bite them when Hitchhiker cuts himself and Franklin and then marks their van with blood. Even at the end of the film, when the truck driver attempts to help Sally, he becomes a target and Leatherface attempts to hurt him. He cuts his losses and drives away, and Sally is lucky enough to jump into the back of a pickup and be carried to safety.

In *Halloween*, Michael becomes the discipliner for the absent parents.[2] Since they aren't there to punish the teens, someone has to be. The only ones who really recognize Michael as the bogeyman are the children that Laurie is babysitting, Tommy and Lindsey, and Laurie herself. The audience first meets Tommy when Laurie is taking the key over to the old Myers place for her father. As she makes her way to the door, Tommy makes a comment that she shouldn't go up there because something bad happened there once. Laurie ignores his childish fears and places the key in the mail slot as instructed. Later, while Tommy is leaving school, he is surrounded and taunted by bullies, who claim that the bogeyman is going to get him. He is actually grabbed and released by Michael, who then returns to stalking Laurie.

As the bogeyman, Michael represents the cultural boundaries that children are not supposed to cross. Tommy believes that the old Myers place is haunted because he is not supposed to enter the premises. Laurie isn't fazed because she knows that demons like that don't exist. When Tommy is being taunted by bullies, Michael shows up and scares them away, thus protecting him from harassment. Michael's main focus is to punish teens who engage in premarital sex. Again, it was a culturally unacceptable act, but since no one else is disciplining the teens, Michael steps in. The kids and Laurie are able to survive their encounter with Michael because all of them still retain their innocence when it comes to sexuality. Unfortunately for Laurie, since she is older and is tempted by sexual situations, she has to fight against Michael to protect herself.

Freddy Krueger makes a great bogey because he attacks the teens in their dreams. Since bogeymen aren't really supposed to exist, this is the perfect place to attack since he can just appear as a creation of the imagination. Like Michael, Freddy's actions are supposed to keep the teens within the boundaries of innocence, away from sexual desires and acts. Unlike Michael, Freddy is not killing because the parents are absent, he is doing it out of revenge and to show the teens the treacherous side of the world, which the parents should have prepared them for but didn't. Although the parents try to protect their kids, they don't do a very good job and often go outside of social boundaries to ensure their safety. This is evident when they decide to take justice in their own hands and kill Freddy.

Nancy's father, the cop in the film, is the last holdout to believe that Freddy is actually attacking the teens. Again, he has to function in the world of evidence and proof, so he is looking for a real killer. At the end of the film, when Nancy has dragged Freddy into the real world, her father has problems believing it, even though he sees the destruction with his own eyes. He leaves the room, and Nancy has to defeat Freddy on her own.

The killers in *Scream* function in the same way as the others. The parents are largely absent, either having left because of an affair (Billy's mom) or are constantly gone on business trips (Sidney's dad). The opening sequence of the film shows Casey getting ready to watch a movie with her boyfriend while her parents are gone. They arrive just as the killer pounces on her, and they hear her grisly death on the phone. Perhaps if they had gotten home five minutes earlier, or hadn't gone out at all, their daughter would still be alive. Despite the fact the brutal murders are happening in town, Stuart's parents still leave, and he plans on having a party at his house. It is at this moment that the vast majority of the murders take place.

In a way, the killers in *Scream* are not only punishing the children, they are punishing the parents. After all, they are the ones who are really acting outside of accepted social boundaries. Billy kills Sidney's mother the year previously for the affair that drove his mother away and framed one of her lovers. His plan for the current murders is to frame Sidney's father. Even the death of the principal reinforces this fact. He is the closest adult to a parental figure and tries to discipline two students for running around the school dressed as the killer. He tries to point out the insensitivity of it all, but later, he puts on the mask and gawks at himself in the mirror. When the students find out he has been hanged on a goalpost, they leave the party to check it out before the cops take him down. The focus of *Scream* is that anyone who is not following accepted social behaviors will be killed.

Like other slasher films, *Scream* has its authority figure that is represented through a cop. Dewey, like all cops in these films, is completely worthless when it comes to fighting the killer. His job is to protect Sidney and her friends, but he can't do that. He gets stabbed in the back by the killer and collapses on the front porch. As usual, the Final Girl has to depend on herself to survive.

Mrs. Voorhees as a bogeyman is a bit more problematic. Even though she functions like the others and is there to punish the teens for behaving outside of social norms, she doesn't have the supernatural presence like the other killers. One of the aspects that make bogeys great literary allegories is their ability to come back. The hero may be able to vanquish them, but they are never down for good. This is evident in *Black Christmas*, *Texas*, *Halloween*, and *Nightmare*. The killer is never found in *Black Christmas*, and Sally never kills Leatherface; she leaves him on the street revving his chain saw. Michael may have been shot and pushed out a window, but he still has the ability to get up and walk away. Freddy can't be vanquished because he doesn't exist in the real world.

Mrs. Voorhees, on the other hand, is decapitated and doesn't physically come back. Her vengeance and notions of revenge are revived in the second film when Jason continues the murders she started. Her influence is symbolized by the presence of her decapitated head in Alice's fridge at the beginning of the movie and on the altar in Jason's shack at the end. Jason fits nicely into the bogeyman ideal because he is very difficult to kill.

The killers in *Scream* are much like Mrs. Voorhees because they can be defeated, but someone else puts on the costume and continues where the murders left off, giving the killer an immortal quality. Even though there is a resolution and the killer is defeated at the end of each of these films, the audience knows they will be coming back. Even though the killers return time after time, the hero or heroine can vanquish them because the killers have to act within a specific set of rules.

The Teachers Are Tough

The actions of the killers can be classified into the allegorical category of obsessive-compulsive behavior because it is constantly repeated and must follow certain rules. Fletcher writes:

> The typical agent in an allegorical fiction has been seen as a daemon, for whom freedom of active choice hardly exists. This appears to have a major correlate in the theory of compulsive behavior, where it is observed that the mind is suddenly obsessed by an idea over which it has no control, which as it were "possesses" the mind. The commonest experience of the compulsive neurotic is that he is suddenly disturbed by impulses that have no apparent rational meaning, and thence are seen as arbitrary and external "commands." It is thus foreignness that is emphasized by psychoanalysts.[3]

The idea of being "possessed" by an idea is symbolized in *Psycho* and *Black Christmas* with the killers being ordered around by their mothers. Both killers have incorporated the personality of an authoritarian female into their psyche, and it is this overbearing voice that drives them to kill. They don't realize it is their own mind that is actually creating the alter ego; they perceive it as an outside, separate command. This is why the killer in *Black Christmas* makes phone calls in a woman's voice after the murders and why Norman dresses like his mother to kill. Even Mrs. Voorhees is influenced by the personality of her dead son. As she is chasing Alice, she speaks in a high-pitched childlike voice that orders her, "Kill her, Mommy."

This possession takes hold of the killers after they have been traumatized and have created conservative ideals and a fictitious past. They are obsessed with the notion that if the teens would have followed their made-up rules, bad things wouldn't have happened.

They focus on teaching the teens a lesson and will not be swayed from their task.

Not all killers incorporate different personalities into their own. In the second *Friday* film, Jason has a habit of keeping his mother's head on an altar and performing the same type of murders as she did, and the family in *Texas* keeps the half-dead corpse of Grandpa around. Outside influences exist that elicit the command for the killers to kill. For Jason, it is done out of revenge, but for the family in *Texas*, it is to keep the tradition of slaughter alive. "Compulsive behavior is highly ordered; it is supersystematic; it is excessively scrupulous, even when no particularly unusual 'ritual' is performed."[4] This is most evident in the way the killer in *Black Christmas* calls the house after each murder, the way in which Leatherface uses tools from the slaughterhouse, the way Michael Myers stalks Laurie and the other victims, in Freddy's torment of the teens in their dreams, and the way in which neither Jason nor his mother rush or become sloppy in their killing sprees. This behavior is repeated throughout the entire series of these films; after the original, the audience is never shocked by the actual deaths, it is just a mystery of where and when they will happen.

The obsessive-compulsive behavior of the killers is further emphasized in the way they are completely focused on one task and one specific age group.

> With imagery our parallel implies much that same sort of narrowing process. It is found with obsessional behavior that the daemonic impulse to perform some irrational act is very soon displaced onto some associatively remote item of imagery. The impulse to kill a loved one is accepted into consciousness by the neurotic mind, because this irrational impulse is attached to some object which is only indirectly associated with that loved person. The typical impulse of this sort becomes frozen into an idée fixe, it becomes compulsion, that is to say, we have the same process in compulsive behaviors that we have already noticed in the case of allegorical imagery: it is often a kind of frozen agency.[5]

The killers target mainly teens, not because they actually wronged them, but because they remind them of the ones who did. There is the potential there that the teens could be bad, so they kill them before they get the chance. They become the killers' "idée fixe," and the obsession is further emphasized in the first-person camera work that occurs in the films. One of the best examples comes from *Halloween*. The audience sees through Michael's eyes as he stalks his prey and then kills them. They never know exactly why he has decided to kill his sister, they can only make assumptions. Maybe he was upset that she didn't take him trick-or-treating; maybe he felt like she was growing up too fast.

Some scholars have postulated that his reaction to seeing his sister have sex is due to the Oedipus complex. According to Vera Dika, author of *Games of Terror*,

> *Halloween* reenacts several thinly disguised elements from Freud's theory: the child's desire to see the sexual activity of the parents; the misinterpretation of those events as violence; and the desire of the child to possess the mother sexually. In *Halloween*, this desire has been displaced onto another close family member (Michael's sister), but much like *Psycho*, the sexual impulse that generates this overvaluation has been transformed into the expression of violent action.[6]

The Oedipus complex definitely explains Norman's motives. He kills because he was jealous of his mother and her lover. He believes his mother would be just as jealous if he had sexual desires for another woman, so he dresses in women's clothes to kill the object of that desire. For Michael, the Oedipus complex may explain why he murders his sister, but it does not explain why he continues to go after teens when he returns home. It is possible he is displacing his desire for his sister onto the others after they have had sex, but why does he go after Laurie? She does not engage in any sexual activity at all; she is the "good girl" who obeys all the rules.

The other killers are not killing a "loved one"; however, the impulse to kill the teens is "indirectly associated" with a loved one. For example, in *Black Christmas*, the killer targets the girls in the sorority because of some fixation he had with his own sister. In *Texas*, the basic drive is the need for food. The family has targeted motorists, hippies in this case, because they are a wandering group that will, more than likely, not be missed by anyone. Mrs. Voorhees kills camp counselors because back in 1957, they let her son drown in Crystal Lake. The teens' irresponsibility and sexuality becomes frozen in her mind, and she uses that to justify the murders of the teens who had nothing to do with Jason's drowning. Jason does the same thing after he kills Alice; he projects his neurosis onto the other teens who had nothing to do with his mother's decapitation or his drowning. The action, or even the image of the teens, engaging in sex or anything fun becomes the only thing these two killers need to push them into a murderous rampage. Freddy goes after the teens whose parents killed him, but also those who are on the edge of innocence. His victims before his death were kids, so he has a fascination with youth. The teens have both childlike and adult-like qualities about them. Billy is obsessed with getting his family back. His main target is Sidney, but he goes after those around her to toy with her. He enjoys watching her pain and discomfort and wants her to feel the loss of those she loves as badly as he does. It's not enough for him that her mother is already dead, he wants her to suffer more.

These obsessive-compulsive behaviors are constantly present throughout the entire series of the different films, and Fletcher claims that within extreme cases of obsessive-compulsive behaviors, "The antisocial impulse that plagues the patient at the same time cries out for an antidote, which it finds in a mental process by which the patient denies his own connection with that impulse."[7] Norman deals with his killings by taking on the personality of his mother. He is so convinced she is a separate entity, he acts surprised and upset when he sees Marion's body. To protect his mother, he cleans up the mess and disposes of the body. The killer in *Black Christmas* stays hidden in the shadows and takes on the personality of a woman when making the phone calls after each murder. By doing this, he wants to make the other sisters aware of what he's done, perhaps even frighten them away since he can't stop killing, but he doesn't confess outright. The family in *Texas* copes with their crimes through their insanity, and Michael separates himself from his murders by hiding behind a mask. Mrs. Voorhees incorporates Jason's personality into her own and has him ordering her to kill the teens. She is trying to separate herself from the crimes she is committing, yet she cannot ignore the compulsion to get revenge. Jason functions in the same manner in part 2, which is why he keeps his mother's head on an altar. This allows him to distance himself from the killings because he can justify, in his mind, that his mother made him do it. Freddy kills for revenge and can only attack in dreams. Billy in *Scream* hides behind a mask like Michael but also has a friend help him kill.

In many ways, the teens themselves are caught in obsessive-compulsive behaviors. The rites of passage dictate that they must behave and perform in certain ways if they are to rejoin society, even if it means acting in ways that go against society's norms. Obsessive-compulsive behavior can also be looked at as a type of ritual act because "compulsive rituals have an infinite number of kinds of materials. Almost any object, any image, any word or words, any icon will do for this purpose, since what makes something a ritual is not a particular substance, but a particular order and repetition of parts."[8] The ritual of obsessive-compulsive behavior comes into play when the Final Characters constantly have to fight to ensure that things change. In the case of *Black Christmas, Halloween, Nightmare,* and *Friday the 13th*, the killers keep trying to push conservative ideals onto the teens, which entails a return to a time when the teens weren't having sex and women knew their place was in the home, and the Final Characters are obsessed with attacking those ideals with liberalism, which means picking up a weapon and defeating the killer.

The purpose of slasher films is to show the conflict between being forced to remain in a static situation or fight against the killers' fictitious lessons from the past, and there is obviously a specific division between the two groups and what they stand for, but only because there is supposed to be. Genre itself can be considered an obsessive-compulsive entity because it mandates actions that must occur within them to be classified into a specific category. There is very little play allowed within a set genre, and slasher films adhere to this ideal. This repetition of patterns also helps to comfort the audience because there is a sense of security in knowing exactly what is going to happen.

The Killers Are Predictable

There must be a basic premise that governs the actions of the killer. The killers are passing on knowledge that they learned from the older generation. According to Fletcher, an authoritarian or parental figure sets a standard of behavior using the strictest authority they can (he uses toilet training as the example in his book, p. 299). He adds,

> The "authoritarian personality," so-called, which closely parallels the compulsive personality, has simply (or not so simply) achieved an "automatization of conscience." When trying to account for the large number of automatized, robotlike characters of moral fable we should examine the degree to which, therefore, there is inherent in their actions some fixed image of conflicting emotions, since the parental figure and the parental command are bound to elicit such emotions.[9]

The killers are supposed to learn from these authority/parental figures and pass that knowledge to the teens. The authority figures in slasher films are supposed to represent the ideal past. Unfortunately, they do not fit into the roles they are supposed to fulfill. Norman's mother was controlling and overbearing. When it suited her needs, she also neglected her son for her own happiness with her lover. The killer's mother in *Black Christmas* seemed to be absent and left him alone with his sister, which led to something awful happening. In *Texas*, there seems to be a complete lack of parental figures. There is Grandpa and "Old Man," the owner/operator of the gas station and Leatherface's older brother, but they are just as crazy as the ones they are supposed to be controlling. In *Halloween*, the parents are largely absent, which may be why Laurie becomes the substitute parental figure. She watches Tommy and eases his fears about monsters and chastises him for his reading material, and she also takes charge of Lindsey, whom Annie is supposed to be watching. When Michael attacks, her first concern is to make sure the children are safe.

The audience does not know exactly what kind of authority Mrs. Voorhees used on her son, they can only see how she punishes the teens around her and assume that she was a strict authoritarian. The parents in *Nightmare* were so overprotective of their children, they committed murder, and then they either run off to Vegas (Tina's mother) or are too engrossed in their jobs to be concerned about their children (Nancy's father). The parents in *Scream* are either away on business trips or having affairs with one another. With the parents largely absent or failing at their jobs, that means Freddy and Billy have to step in and be the parental figures, which is detrimental. Neither one of them have children of their own. Billy is too young, and Freddy murdered them. The same scenario applies to Jason. How is he supposed to represent parental authority when he never was one?

For most of these killers, there is very little conflicting emotion. Most parents, when they discipline their children, feel torn because they have to do something that hurts their child, such as a spanking or a stern scolding. The majority of parents don't like to see their kids in physical or emotional pain, but the children have to be taught a lesson. The killers in slasher films don't really care if they inflict physical or emotional pain. They are trying to control the teens' actions and use any means necessary to get their point across.

These actions don't only apply to individual films, they carry throughout the series. For example, Mrs. Voorhees set the basic premise for how the teens in the film would be killed, and Jason follows her actions almost exactly. Some of Mrs. Voorhees's most memorable murders are copied in *Friday the 13th Part 2* with very little variation. These examples can be seen in the death of Jack, from the first film, who is stabbed through the neck from under the bed. Jason uses this in the second film on Jeff and Sandra, but attacks them from above while they are in the middle of sex, not after, and he impales both of them to the bed. Marcie's famous death, with the ax in the face, is also repeated in the second film when Jason kills Mark, the teen in the wheelchair, with his machete. Like Marcie, he is whacked across the face, but it is done outside, and he then proceeds to roll down the stairs of the cabin. Aside from these major types of deaths, throat slitting and characters being stabbed are rampant throughout the entire series. As Jason gets stronger, deaths inflicted by hand, such as neck breaking and head crushing, become common elements and begin repeating through the later films.

Throughout the series of *Nightmare* films, Freddy attacks teens in their dreams. The location changes (i.e., the third film takes place in an asylum), but the murders stay the same. Same situation in *Scream*: even though Billy and Stuart are dead, a new killer is willing to pick up where they left off and continue torturing Sidney. The slight variations that do occur in these films are only there to keep the audience interested (just like adding more deaths to the films), but the repetition of the murders reinforces how static the situation is that these killers are operating in; they can't even vary their patterns of how they kill the teens.

The authoritarian figure is the driving force behind ritual. Ritual is very repetitive, but it is also supposed to allow the culture to pass on wisdom, values, and morals from one generation to the next. This is prominently displayed within the family from *Texas*. Psychosis is not just a problem that one of the family members has to deal with, all of them have been immersed in the sickness.

The audience can only assume the traits were passed down from one generation to the next. The audience also knows, courtesy of Hitchhiker, that he and his grandfather both worked in the slaughterhouse before it was shut down. We can also assume Leatherface had some contact with the killing of cows because of the way he dispatches of the teens. Since they no longer have the slaughterhouse to work in, they have put their skills to different use. This would also explain why Sally's pleas for her life have no effect on the family. When she tells them she would do anything if they would let her go, implying sexual favors, they don't get the point. They don't view her as a human, they view her as an animal. She is their next source of food and nothing more.

Norman learned from his mother that desire can be a dangerous emotion. When she found another lover, he felt abandoned. To make up for his sense of loss and to appease his jealousy, he murdered his mother and her lover in their bed and incorporated her personality into his. He murders women he is sexually attracted to because he believes his mother would feel just as abandoned and jealous if he were to find a lover.

The ritual for the killer in *Black Christmas* is difficult to ascertain since the audience doesn't know exactly what happened to his sister. We know he feels a sense of loss and tries to use Clare's corpse as a replacement, but what drove him to that situation is a mystery. When he makes his phone calls after each murder and speaks in the female's voice, it is evident that she is very upset and may have been abusive. If that is the case, it would explain his brutal murders of the other girls. His hatred or fear of the female authority figure would have been passed down to him through her actions.

For Michael, ritual is not passed down from one generation to the next but carried throughout several years. His hatred of teens who have sex stays with him as he lives in the asylum and then when he escapes. The teens cannot protect themselves from his wrath because they don't even know he exists until it is too late. Even when Laurie is able to defeat him, she doesn't come out of the ordeal unscathed; and he vanishes, presumably to continue the process of punishing teens who participate in sexual activity.

Ritual succeeding from one generation to the next would explain why Jason mimics his mother's behavior, and Jason functions mechanically because he is being controlled by a static society that he has no desire of leaving. This would also explain the few times the audience sees Jason with any "conflicting emotion," which is symbolized in his reduction to a child, and this occurs when the teens are able to subdue him psychologically.

This is most evident in the second film when Ginny is able to make him believe that she is his mother. Obsessive-compulsive behavior is driven by external commands that make the subject feel anxious if the actions are not carried out. Mrs. Voorhees is the symbolic representation of the ideals that dictate how Jason behaves; Ginny is able to recognize this and trick Jason into believing she is the authoritarian figure he must obey. She accomplishes this by dressing in Mrs. Voorhees's sweater and speaking in a tone Jason recognizes as being authoritative, which is why he submits and goes down to his knees. Unfortunately, when Ginny raises the machete to strike, she not only reveals Mrs. Voorhees's head, but reinforces how her behavior differs from the static world Jason acts in, and this is enough to put him back on the offensive and injure her. If Ginny had been able to remain in the static, ritual behaviors that define Jason's actions, she might have had a better chance of keeping Jason fooled, but the whole conflict between the two characters revolves around the fact that Ginny wants change and will act violently to get it.

The wisdom that was supposed to be passed down in *Nightmare* was how to defeat Freddy, but since the parents believed they already took care of him, they kept the information to themselves. They probably thought they were protecting their kids by not telling them about Fred Krueger, but when he first started attacking, they should have told them the story instead of pretending it wasn't happening. The failure of the elder generation to pass this wisdom on is what dooms the teens. They have no way to defeat the killer, so he conquers them.

The failure to communicate between generations also exists in *Scream*. In this film, the parents are too busy running around and having affairs or traveling on business trips, and they don't realize how their actions are affecting their children. This is evident in the scene between Sidney and Gale when they are talking about Cotton. Sidney had testified that he was the man who murdered her mother, but Gale did some investigative reporting and figured out that he wasn't the actual killer. When confronted by this news, Sidney realizes she may have been mistaken. Then, when Billy confesses to the murders, she knows she was mistaken. Sidney didn't want to believe her mother was having an affair, so she viewed Cotton as an intruder. Since no other parent stepped in to correct her, she doomed an innocent man. For the other teens in the films, since no parental figure is there to help them with the killer, they have to get their wisdom from old slasher movies, and that doesn't save them.

Ritual is an act passed down to the subject by an elder figure that must be followed properly if the individual is going to function within society. The killers in slasher films function as this elder, and they have become obsessed with trying to control the teens. They view the teens as troublemakers who are constantly getting in trouble with the law, but societal law in the movies doesn't punish them. The killers obsessively watch the teens, waiting for them to screw up, and when they do, the killers jump at the opportunity to punish them.

Be Wary of Your Surroundings

The killer as a demon teacher ties into the notion that the killer is an elder who is supposed to teach the teens the proper way to act when they become adults. This idea can still be applied when looking at the killer as a symbolic representation of society. Victor Turner, author of *The Ritual Process*, describes this ritual as an act that is constantly repeated within a society, generally a tribal society, that is static and mostly unchanged.[10] For the most part, this applies to the films because the teens are being taught how to function in a very ritualistic way with certain rules that must be followed. On the other hand, it doesn't work exactly the way it is supposed to. The greatest example of this is the way in which the killer uses murder to punish the teens. Turner has never observed in his anthropological studies an "initiand" being killed for doing something wrong; one may be severely punished but still make it back to society. Also, Turner never recorded a ritual subject fighting against and killing an elder, which means that these films are not showing how well the killers pass on wisdom, but how they have failed. This is the reason the Final Girl never returns to society: there is no static society to return to, only one that is constantly changing. The Final Girl fights back against the killer because she doesn't want to be a part of his obsessive, repetitive, controlling, and fictitious world. The demonic villain constantly keeps coming back to try and make her, which leads them into an unending conflict.

The setting of these films plays an important role in the passing of wisdom, mainly because it takes the teens out of a changing society and places them into a static one. The setting for the *Friday* movies, a summer camp, aside from being a socially loaded place associated with fun and away from social schedules, is also a place that is only visited once a year, and it is a place that really never changes over time. Summer camps, generally, have very little technological amenities, such as running water and electricity, and those that do have rudimentary systems, and that makes them a great representation for the many tribal societies that practice the rites of passage for their adolescents.

Camp Crystal Lake was first established in 1935 and functioned up until 1958 when the two camp counselors were murdered. There had been several attempts to reopen the camp, but they were always thwarted by Mrs. Voorhees, who would set fires or poison the water (this was never proven, only assumed when the camp was found to have "bad" water). Her son had drowned a year before the first murders, and Mrs. Voorhees wants to keep the camp frozen in time. Any change that might occur to the place has to be stopped, and Mrs. Voorhees does this by killing anyone who gets in the way. When the teens show up again to reopen the camp, she murders them when she gets the chance, but the tribal-like setting and the ritual that surrounds the teens while they are there cannot stop change, and this happens when the Final Girl fights back and kills the killer.

The Bates Motel is off the main highway on a road that doesn't see a lot of traffic. Like a summer camp, a motel is a place people don't stay in for very long. Motels are generally associated with vacations and the sense of getting away from it all. They generally are equipped with basic amenities to ensure the patrons are comfortable. Although the Bates Motel isn't visited often by guests, Norman makes sure he changes the bedding once a week whether it's been slept in or not. His world is very static and hardly changes. The only change that occurs for him is after the murder of Marion. Not only does he have to dispose of the body and all evidence she was there, he has to lie to the myriad of people who are looking for her. His static, unchanging world is upset by the appearance of Arbogast, Sam, and Lila, and he doesn't know how to deal with that change, which is why he gets caught.

Sally's grandparents' house in *Texas* is run down and lacking technology, and according to Sally, it also was never visited on a regular basis. The Leatherface family's house is also another static location. The floors are littered with the relics of the past, such as bones from previous victims, and Grandma is kept as a mummy in her rocking chair. Although the slaughterhouse has closed and everyone has been laid off, this does not stop the family from continuing to do their job. They've replaced cattle with people, but little else has changed. The watch hanging from the tree with a nail driven through it symbolizes how time has stopped or has been forced to stop. But since nothing can remain static forever and change is bound to happen, Leatherface's tantrum at the end of the film when Sally gets away shows that something has changed in their world. Since he has no concept of how to deal with that change, his reaction is to angrily rev his chain saw. This change is an uneasy revelation because the killer is never vanquished.

The setting of *Black Christmas* takes place at a sorority house on a university campus. This setting is outside of social boundaries because it is constructed to be a town all its own. Students generally have everything they need while attending school. Since the majority of their time is spent going to classes or studying, there really isn't much besides warmth and food that needs to be provided to them. Colleges and universities also function outside of accepted social boundaries because of the freedom granted to the students (see lesson 3 for a more in-depth discussion on this). Even the sisters in the house have separated themselves from the "townies." Since they are paying for school and acquiring a higher education, some of them feel like they are better than those who live off campus. Change occurs when the outside world threatens the home, which happens when the killer climbs into the attic and murders the girls.

Even the killer feels threatened when something from outside invades his space. This is evident in the tantrum he throws after he murders Mrs. Mac. She makes her way into the attic while looking for the cat, with the taxicab driver honking his horn on the street, and just happens to discover Clare's body. Since the killer feels threatened, he kills her with a hook and pulley. He then glances out the window, anxiously awaiting the departure of the cabbie. When he leaves, the killer then proceeds to have a fit. He was content to kill at his own will, but she invaded his space and upset his ritual.

Nothing has really changed for Michael except his choice of victim. Even after fifteen years of being in the asylum, he is able to return home and find it still standing. Granted, his family has moved out, but the neighborhood remains largely the same. No one talks about what happened on that dreadful Halloween night in 1963, with the exception of Tommy, who believes it is nothing more than a scary story. Haddonfield has remained static, just like Michael; parents are still absent and teens are still having premarital sex. Michael returns to do what he's always done: punish teens. It would appear that his return upsets the static nature of the town, but no one knows he's there. It is Dr. Loomis's presence and Laurie that upset the ritual. Dr. Loomis upsets it by trying to stop Michael, and Laurie fights back, something the other victims didn't do. If the doctor hadn't intervened and Laurie hadn't wounded him, Michael would have carried out his obsessive-compulsive behaviors unhindered.

Freddy operates in the world of dreams. Every individual experiences dreams differently. Some people are very vivid dreamers, while others can't remember them. Even though dreaming seems like an individual experience, it is actually a very static state. Dreams can only occur when you are asleep. Freddy cannot come after his victims when they are awake. Unfortunately, since no one can stay awake forever, he usually gets his chance to go after his victims. He is so powerful in the dream world that the teens die in the real world. Change occurs when Nancy pulls Freddy out of the dream world. Since he is no longer functioning in a static state, he can be easily vanquished by Nancy turning her back on him. However, this does not defeat him. He still exists in the dream world and continues to murder teens.

Like *Halloween*, the teens in *Scream* are in a static suburban setting. The only thing that upsets their idyllic neighborhood is the murders, which brings in news crews from all across the country. But even then, there is an attempt to keep life going on as usual. The kids still go to school (until it is shut down by the police) and they still have parties. They still engage in underage drinking and premarital sex. The killers count on these things remaining static to continue their torment of Sidney. What upsets this ritual is the others who survive (Gale and Randy) who help Sidney overcome the killers.

The teens in these films are in a fixed position, unable to move to any other place, much like the killers.

The teens of *Scream* (1996): Skeet Ulrich, Neve Campbell, Matthew Lillard, Rose Mc-Gowan, Jamie Kennedy. *Dimension Films/Photofest © Dimension Films*

This, I think, is the case with all allegorical agents, and when an author is interested in what seem to be free metamorphoses and changes of state, he is in fact not showing his characters acting freely. He is showing them changing, presto, from one facet of destiny to another. They remain bound to the Wheel of Fortune, though it turns, rising and falling to give them the illusion of a changed state. . . . The idea that the hero undergoes a change as a result of a psychomachia in which he battles, or of an agony, a progress, a voyage to the moon, or whatever typical story we choose, should not blind us to the real lack of freedom in all these stories. . . . These heroes do not choose, then do not "deliberate" but act on compulsion, continually demonstrating a lack of inner control.[11]

This fixed position plays through all of the films, as they are constantly going through and repeating the same situations over and over again. Even when the teens believe they are making drastic alterations, Jason, Michael, Leatherface, Freddy, or Norman come back and try to control their every action.

How to Survive

The Final Characters in these films are trapped in a very repetitive world where they must follow certain rules if they are to survive. Fletcher writes,

> It becomes possible to predict what is going to happen in allegories. With our analogy in hand we learn to look afresh at the mode. In both cases, therefore, we find an authorian sort of behavior, rigid, anxious, fatalistic; the hero of an allegorical epic will be presented to us doing things the way a compulsive person does things, regularly, meticulously, blindly. In both cases there is great play for magical influence, psychic possession, taboo restrictions. In both cases we shall expect events to be isolated from each other into highly episodic forms, thereby "encapsulating" particular moments of contagion and beatitude.[12]

These rules are present in all of the films, are set up by the killers, and revolve around their actions. The Final Characters must follow the ritual, which generally involves not acting against the killer until all the friends are dead and the bodies have popped out in front of them. Once that happens, the Final Character must then go through the ritual of fear and try to hide from the killer. This then leads to the acknowledgment that she cannot escape the killer, and only then is she able to pick up a weapon to defend herself. Like the formula that classifies slasher films into their genres, the characters have a formula they must follow if they are to be categorized as Final Characters.

Lila in *Psycho* seems to be outside of this formula since she never picks up a weapon to defeat Norman, but she isn't. Her persistence and stubbornness to find out what happened to her sister and Detective Arbogast force her to go to the Bates Motel. Once there, she needs to get inside the house, so she forces Sam to keep Norman busy. She pokes through Mrs. Bates's room, noticing that everything has its place but realizing something is off, then decides to head back downstairs. It is at this point that Norman comes into the house, and Lila has to hide from him. She doesn't find the body of her sister or the detective, but she does find the body of Mrs. Bates. Norman then attacks her, and she is saved by Sam. Even though she doesn't save herself, the outcome is the same and the killer is defeated.

After the indecent phone calls in *Black Christmas* are reported to the police, it becomes Jess's task to keep the guy on the line for as long as possible to trace the call. Jess has no idea that her friends have been murdered. It isn't until the police figure out the calls are coming from inside the house and try to get her to leave that she realizes the danger she is in. Of course, instead of leaving, she grabs a fireplace poker and goes upstairs to investigate, only to find her dead friends and to be attacked by the killer. She is able to get away and hides in the basement, where she is found by Peter. Fearing he is the killer, she attacks and kills him. Unfortunately, since he wasn't the killer and the real murderer is lurking in the attic, there are implications that she doesn't survive.

Sally and her brother Franklin wait impatiently by their van for the rest of their friends to return, unaware they have been butchered by Leatherface. When she decides to go looking for her boyfriend, she is forced to take Franklin with her. As she struggles to push his wheelchair over the uneven and overgrown terrain, they are attacked by Leatherface. Franklin is killed, but Sally makes it to the gas station, where the attendant claims he will take her to find help. Little does she know, it is Old Man, and he takes her back to the house. She passes out on the way, and when she regains consciousness, she is tied to a chair and the torment begins. Sally realizes the predicament she is in, and has to flee if she wants to survive. She never personally kills any of her attackers, but Hitchhiker is lured onto the highway while pursuing her and run over by a semi. The driver gets out of the cab to see what is going on, and finds Sally, bloody and screaming for help with Leatherface right behind her. He throws a wrench at Leatherface and hits him in the side of the head, causing him to fall and cut his leg with his chain saw. The driver doesn't wait around for much longer, and drives off without Sally. His intervention, though, gives her enough time to climb into another truck and be taken to safety.

Laurie knows that Michael is stalking her before she realizes he is the killer. She first sees him while sitting in English after glancing out the window. She stares at him for a while then turns back to answer a question posed by the teacher. When she looks back out the window, he is gone. As Laurie and her friends are walking home, Michael drives by in the car he stole from the asylum. Both Lynda and Annie think it is a cute boy from school, so they yell after him, causing Michael to slam on the brakes before taking off again. Laurie tries to tell them that she doesn't think it's Devon Graham, but it doesn't really matter to her friends. As she and Annie continue home, Laurie again sees Michael at the end of the block. He ducks behind a bush, and Laurie mentions it to Annie, who immediately runs to check it out. Annie jokes that the boy behind the bush wants to take Laurie out on a date, but when Laurie gets there, no one is there. Even when she finally gets home, while up in her room, she looks out the window to see Michael in the neighbors' yard. By this point in time, it would have been wise for Laurie to call someone and let them know she was being stalked, but when Michael disappears again, she puts him out of her mind. Of course, she has no reason to believe he is there to cause harm. For all she knows, it is some kid from school playing a prank. Later that night, after a phone call from Lynda, she heads over to the neighbors' house to figure out what is going on and finds the bodies of her friends. She is distressed and realizes she has to do something but doesn't take physical action until Michael threatens her life and the lives of the children she is babysitting. To fight him off, she has to stab him with a knitting needle, poke him in the eye with a hanger, and eventually have him shot by Dr. Loomis. This only happens after attempting to hide from Michael. He keeps finding her, and she has no choice but to fight back to survive.

Alice, from *Friday the 13th*, fits very nicely into this formula also. She doesn't seem to be too concerned that all of her friends have suddenly disappeared. She and Bill make an attempt to look for them and try to leave to get help, but when that fails, she heads back to the main lodge and falls asleep on the couch. It is only when she finds Bill's body impaled to a door and Brenda's body comes crashing through the window into the kitchen that she makes a serious attempt to get away from the camp. She then runs into Mrs. Voorhees and discovers she is the murderer. Alice knocks her out, hides herself in the pantry, where she is discovered, and then runs off toward the lake. Mrs. Voorhees discovers her there, and, not having anyplace else to go, Alice fights back and chops off the killer's head.

In *Nightmare*, Nancy is concerned about Tina's nightmare and agrees to stay the night with her, but she isn't too concerned until she finds out they both had the same nightmare. When she figures out the nightmare can actually kill her and she sees Tina's mutilated body, she takes steps to protect herself. She attempts to hide from Freddy by not falling asleep, but since she can't stay awake forever, she devises a plan. She hopes Glen and her father will be able to help her, but when they fail, she takes matters into her own hands.

Sidney is chased and taunted by the murderer throughout the film. She tries to prove she's not afraid of him by calling his bluff, stepping out onto the porch to face him, but when he comes after her, she always runs. She is chased through her house, stalked in the school's bathroom, and attacked at the party at Stuart's house. At the party, she finds Tatum's body hanging from the garage door, Dewey gets stabbed in the back in front of her, and she finally has to confront the killer. She uses his method and calls him on the phone, changing her voice. She even dresses in the same costume and jumps out of a closet. The only difference between her and other Final Girls is that she uses a gun to deliver the fatal blow. However, the result is the same, and she defeats the killer.

The rules and formula that are applied to the Final Characters have the ability to be played with, and the producers change elements, such as having a boy as the surviving character or by having more than one character live. The few alterations that occur in these films are both for the benefit of the audience, keeping the film fresh and interesting, and as a representation of how the teens in society have to change their course of action to reach their goals. Leatherface, Jason, Michael, and the other killers never have to change their actions because they are trapped in ideals from the past, while the teens are trying to progress with the times. They will do anything and fight violently to ensure they survive so they can enact some type of social change.

The very fact that the Final Characters pick up weapons to fight against the killer point to how serious they are about changing their society; it is also important to look at the weapons they use and what the implications are behind these choices. The killers in these films use weapons that facilitate the need for them to get close to the victims to kill them. The choice of the Final Character to use the same type of weapon against the killer shows how close they need to get to the killer to defeat them. The premise of ritual is to pass knowledge from one generation to the next, and, despite how hard this system tries, the teens refuse to be a part of the repetition. By picking up a machete or any other type of stabbing instrument, the defeat of the killer is symbolic of the teens' ability to take the lessons taught by the earlier generations, turn it back on them, and show how destructive those actions really are.

The ritual act of passing knowledge from one generation to the next also fails because the authority figures were never part of society. If the focus is supposed to be on the nuclear family, then Norman and his mother don't fit in because they were missing a father. Even when a male was present, he didn't marry Mrs. Bates, thus going against social norms. Their contact with society is brief and done in the context of a business transaction. The hotel is off the main road and doesn't get a lot of customers. Norman does know how to act in the presence of others, but only for brief amounts of time. In his conversation with Marion, he says things that make her uncomfortable, especially when talking about his mother. When Arbogast questions him, he becomes flustered and stutters. By the time Sam enters the office to question him and he realizes Lila is in the house, Norman gives up acting normally and knocks Sam out with a vase. Even his hobby of stuffing birds is out of the ordinary, and Norman's desire to be with his mother keeps him away from other people and in the house with her corpse.

The family in *Texas* would not be the ideal nuclear family because there are no women present, except for the skeleton of Grandma. Perhaps if there was a feminine, nurturing presence, the men wouldn't be so violent. The only idea of femininity in the family is present at dinner when Sally is tied to the chair. Leatherface has changed his mask and clothes into those of a woman. He wears a dress and a mask with makeup as he prepares the family meal. But the audience knows from his earlier actions in the film that he is anything but nurturing. There is also the conversation between Hitchhiker and Old Man, who claims that he cannot kill, that he doesn't have the stomach for it. Hitchhiker mocks him and snidely comments that is why he is just a cook, a role traditionally occupied by a woman. Although he occupies a feminine position and is mocked by the other members of the family, it doesn't make him any less dangerous—or sane.

For the family, it doesn't seem like they have had much contact with society, either. When the group first picks up Hitchhiker, it is apparent he doesn't know how to act around people. His dress and actions suggest an antisocial personality. Most people don't wear a pouch made out of a dead animal as everyday apparel, ritualistically burn pictures of people after they refuse to buy it, or cut themselves without batting an eye. Leatherface seems to have no contact with people except for those he kills. In a scene after he murders Jerry, he paces around the room, wringing his hands and glancing out the window with concern. At first, it seems he might be upset about killing the three teens, but as the film progresses further, the audience

The Leatherface family (John Dugan, seated; Jim Siedow; Gunnar Hensen; Edwin Neal) in *The Texas Chain Saw Massacre* (1974). *New Line Cinema/Photofest © New Line Cinema*

realizes he has no remorse about his murders. When they look back on the action, it wasn't remorse, but concern there might be more people. He was overwhelmed by the fact that the kids surprised him. After Jerry's visit, Leatherface no longer stays in the house but actually goes out to hunt his prey.

The only member of the family that has contact with society is Old Man, and the audience knows he doesn't have the stomach or the ability to kill anyone. Because he owns the gas station and deals with customers on a short-term basis, he is able to turn on normal behavior for short periods of time. When placed in a situation for too long, he devolves into a psychopath, which is apparent when he comes home from a long day at work.

The killer in *Black Christmas* doesn't fit because his family has been destroyed by tragedy. What happened to him afterward is a mystery. His contact with society is limited, if he has any at all, and he sneaks into the sorority house and hides in the attic, only coming down to claim another victim. The only time he attempts to speak to the girls is on the phone, where he scares them and speaks in several different voices. Even though he doesn't have a lot of contact with society, he knows enough to evade capture.

For Michael, the only parental-like figure we see is his sister, and she is way too involved with her own gratification to be concerned about him. Would things have turned out differently if the parents were present? It can be argued that Michael's fascination with Tommy and Laurie stems from the fact that he sees what might have been if he had a mother figure around. Even if Michael identifies with Tommy, there is no way he can return to the past and change it. He also might be fascinated with Laurie's "good mother quality," but that doesn't stop him from trying to kill her.

Freddy never had a family of his own and was content to destroy others by murdering their children. He was a member of society at one time, but he was a destructive force. He knew how to manipulate the system and evaded incarceration for his crimes because of a technicality. He was set free because someone forgot to sign the search warrant. This, of course, leads the parents to take the law into their own hands. This action, along with divorced parents, reinforces how the nuclear family has dissolved.

Billy had a nuclear family until it was destroyed by an affair. After that, like Norman, he felt abandoned. From what he says, he seems to have functioned like a normal teenager until his mother left. After her departure, his focus turned to revenge. He tries to continue to act like a normal teenager, climbing in Sidney's window and wanting to have sex, but it is all a means to an end. He only does it to throw Sidney off his trail so that he can continue to murder. He even tries to pin the murders on Sidney's father and goes so far as to stab himself and Stuart so it looks like they are the only survivors of a heinous attack.

Ritual, here, fails for the killers because they were never able to function in society at all. The killers' antisocial status allows them to undermine the rules and regulations that govern society, thus their unemotional murdering sprees. The only hope in these movies of destroying these demons is that the Final Character is able to figure out the boundaries the killers are operating within and be incorporated into that system. The conflicts between the teens and the killers, society and the teens, and between society and the killers reinforce how horribly ritual has failed. There was never a static society that was teaching the teens how to function as adults, only the hope for one, and that is why the Final Characters or the killers never make it back—the culture is constantly changing. When society does attempt to step in, which is symbolized in the figures of police officers, it is usually after the fact and too late to help the teens.

Conclusion

The goal of society is to pass its values, morals, and ideals on to the next generation. This allows the society to remain static and unchanged. The process involves the younger generation learning from the older generation and not questioning any of the lessons. But when the younger generation refuses to learn and incorporate the lessons from the teacher, society forces their ideals upon them. This is where slasher films come into play. The killers represent society and their desire to return to an idealized past. It is also the killers' role to punish the teens for acting outside accepted social boundaries.

Their actions are obsessive, compulsive, driven by outside forces, and ritualistic. If the teens want to survive their encounter with the killer, they have to incorporate themselves into the system and use the same deadly force against their oppressor.

Notes

1. Angus Fletcher, *Allegory: The Theory of a Symbolic Mode* (Ithaca, N.Y.: Cornell University Press, 1964), 40–41.

2. "Michael functions as the punitive bogeyman that stands in for the disciplining parental figure. Meyers watches the teenagers of Haddonfield more closely than their largely absent parents, he judges their naughty behavior more severely, and he punishes with extreme prejudice. The appearance of Michael Meyers, however, can be read as corresponding not only to the teenagers' wicked behavior but also to the absence of their parents. It is, in a way, the absence of the disciplining parents that calls forth the monstrous bogeyman." Kendall R. Phillips, "*The Exorcist* (1973) and *The Texas Chainsaw Massacre* (1974)," in *Projected Fears: Horror Films and American Culture* (Westport, Conn.: Praeger, 2005), 138.

3. Fletcher, *Allegory*, 286–87.

4. Fletcher, *Allegory*, 291.

5. Fletcher, *Allegory*, 289.

6. Vera Dika, *Games of Terror:* Halloween, Friday the 13th, *and the Films of the Stalker Cycle.* (London: Associated University Presses, 1990), 42.

7. Fletcher, *Allegory*, 290.

8. Fletcher, *Allegory*, 292.

9. Fletcher, *Allegory*, 300.

10. Victor Turner, *The Ritual Process: Structure and Anti-Structure* (New York: Aldine De Gruyter, 1995).

11. Fletcher, *Allegory*, 63–64.

12. Fletcher, *Allegory*, 302.

LESSON THREE
LEARN FROM YOUR MISTAKES

O ne of the most recurring themes in these films, aside from the gruesome murders, is the use of teens as the main characters. This is important because of the social significance of the teenage years, which are generally the most awkward yet one of the most important phases of life. The high school and early college years are most often described as "the best years of your life." Why is that? Teenagers are usually seen as an in-between group because they are no longer children, but they are not yet adults; they are trapped in a place where they are ambiguous. Yet, in this ambiguous phase, there is a freedom of movement, with the teenager trying to figure out who he or she is as a person. It is the perfect phase for society to teach teens the skills they will need to function as adults. In this sense, the teen years can be looked upon as a rite of passage into adult society.

Many tribal societies have used rites of passage to prepare their teens for the adult world, and Victor Turner is an anthropologist who has studied how it occurs in a tribal setting. His works are based on his studies that he conducted at University College of London and on his research he did in Northern Rhodesia while living and studying the Ndembu tribe. Turner's works that were used for this book include *The Ritual Process: Structure and Anti-Structure* and

From Ritual to Theatre: The Human Seriousness of Play, which you can access for further reading and a more in-depth, anthropological discussion on the rites of passage.

Stick Together

One of the most important phases in the rite of passage is being separated from normal society. The separation in slasher films doesn't always mean the teens leave society completely, although sometimes they do. To function as adults, teens need to learn how to fend for themselves and problem solve. The only way they can learn those skills is by being separated from parents. They need to be in a place where they are allowed choices and freedom of movement. They also have to be in a place where normal concepts of time don't exist; it has to feel "out of time."[1]

In *Psycho*, the Bates Motel is off the main highway, outside of normal social boundaries and laws. While the townspeople know about Norman and his family, they don't venture to the motel to see him. Even when Sam and Lila tell the sheriff about Marion and Arbogast, he doesn't actually question Norman face-to-face, he calls him on the phone and just takes his word as gospel. The out-of-time notion comes into play with Norman and his mother. She has been dead for ten years, yet Norman acts like she is still there. All the objects in her room haven't been touched and are probably in the exact spot she left them. Even her indentation on the bed is still in place. Norman himself seems to be out of time because he tries to act as both dutiful son and responsible adult. Then, throw into the mix taking on his mother's personality, and it's hard to know exactly what generation Norman exists in.

The setting of *Black Christmas* takes place on a university campus in a sorority house. This is outside of normal social boundaries because students are allowed certain freedoms. For example, they are expected to get good grades and a degree, but they are also allowed to party and experiment with sexuality. This is why the sergeant at the police station isn't too concerned with finding Clare when her friends and father report her missing. He is convinced (and more than likely has seen it happen before) she is with some boy and will show up later. After all, this is usually the first time the teens have been away from their parents, and they are allowed to go a little crazy. However, the expectation is that they will stop those behaviors once they earn their degree. There are still rules that exist at the university, but in the context of the film, the enforcer is worthless. Mrs. Mac is supposed to make sure the girls have high morals and get good grades, but she doesn't really care. It's not that she doesn't like the girls—she does—but she puts her own needs ahead of others'. The out-of-time aspect comes into play because campuses usually have been around for a long time and don't change very often. Plus, generation after generation will attend the school. More than likely, students will act the same as the ones before and use the opportunity to explore themselves and those around them, much like the girls in the film have done.

In *Texas*, the teens are traveling outside of normal, comfortable boundaries to check on the family graves. The out-of-time experience occurs as they travel across the countryside and see dried crops, skinny cows, and exhumed corpses posed in offensive positions. There is nothing about the landscape that the audience would recognize as Texas. The only reason they know that's where the characters are is because they are told. Some other clues that place the movie in an out-of-time perspective is the portrayal of the teens as hippies. While the year is 1963, no one else around them seems to be a part of the young generation. They seem to have found the only part of the state where teenagers don't exist. They also keep track of time by following astrological symbols and talking about how the planets align. Since they have no jobs or school they need to return to, there is no need for them to worry about time like the rest of the world. This is especially evident when they are in Sally and Franklin's family house. When Sally takes her friends on a tour, she tells them stories of what it was like when she was a child. They don't seem to realize the place is falling down around them and nothing from her childhood remains.

In *Halloween*, there is no physical separation from society. The teens are forced to operate within the boundaries of their neighborhood and homes, but there are no parents around to make sure they obey the rules. The murders also occur within private homes, which, even though they are part of society as a whole, have a sense of sacredness to them because no family is like another; each one has their own schedules and rituals when it comes to daily life, and the home is supposed to be safe. No matter what happens in the outside world, going home should be the one place where you can truly be yourself without being judged. There is no sense of time in this film because the murder Michael committed as a child is being repeated as an adult. The crimes also happen on Halloween, which is a holiday that celebrates the return of the dead to the realm of the living. Time has no meaning because old and new are able to walk freely on the earth.

This notion of separation is evident in the setting of the first two *Friday the 13th* films, which takes place at a summer camp. Usually, summer camps are thought of as a place to get away from the normal, mundane activities of everyday life. Children and counselors are allowed to feel a sense of freedom here because they don't have to worry about school or schedules or even having many adults around. They are allowed to explore themselves and others without a fear of class standings or repercussions from parents or teachers. There is a sense of "going back to nature" with no influence from the outside world. The audience and characters can relate to the summer camp because it is an ideal place that is safe from the horrors of the "real world."

The summer camp is out of time because time seems to be suspended, and the audience is never really sure how long the teens are there—could be a day, could be two. The characters never worry about what day it is or how long they have been there, either. The only passage of time is indicated by day turning into night. There are no set schedules of when things need to be done, and there is a sense of endlessness to their situation.

In *A Nightmare on Elm Street*, dreams are supposed to be a unique and private place for an individual to go. In many cases, the individual doesn't have control over what he or she sees in their mind's eye. It is a normal process that has to happen if we are going to function normally. There is a sacredness to dreams because it transports us to different places or allows us to be different people and live out our fantasies. Normally, it is a safe place to retreat from the pressures and stress of the real world. Even if we experience nightmares, we know they aren't real and can't hurt us. Dreams are out of time because they transport us anywhere. Even though dreams only occur while we're sleeping, which usually occurs at a set time at night, we aren't usually aware of or concerned with the passage of time while dreaming. Freddy is out of time because he's dead and only exists in dreams, and he shows up when and where he wants.

Like *Halloween*, *Scream* functions in the boundaries of suburbia. Again, the home is supposed to be a safe place where the outside world can't harm you. One of the focuses of this film is Sidney's circle of friends. Since her mother is gone and her father is always traveling, Sidney only has her friends to make her feel safe. She stays at Tatum's house after she leaves the police station and is treated like a member of the family. Like the home, being with friends is supposed to be an accepting, nonjudgmental safe haven. Also like *Halloween*, there are not a lot of parents around to keep an eye on their children. The out-of-time notion comes into play when the murders occur. Sidney has tried for a year to put the death of her mother behind her, but with the new killings and the influx of reporters, it is like she is experiencing déjà vu.

Along with separation from normal society, the rite of passage involves a transition phase.[2] During this phase, the teens become ambiguous. Social definitions do not apply to them. It is during this phase that the ritual participants learn the most important aspects of functioning in the adult world.

Have an Identity Crisis

Gender is part of the negotiation in a rite of passage that these teens have to go through. In all of these movies, the teenagers are separated from normal society and all the classifications that society uses to define them. They are in a new place where social boundaries and rules do not exist, and the teens are allowed to explore freely. Notions of hierarchy are dissolved, and teens form intense friendships that are not based on rank or status as society would define them. There is a sense of equality among the group of teens.[3] The role of gender in slasher films is a contentious issue, and one that Carol Clover and Vera Dika have written extensively on. They claim that misogynistic ideals are reinforced within slasher films.

Dika's argument focuses on the humiliation of the women in the film and how everything about the story reinforces men's place in society. She even goes so far as to say: "The wounds are carefully designed to be manifestly seen by the audience, looked at for a while, but not studied for too long. In our assumption that they unconsciously signify the female genitalia, the sight of the bleeding wound, these particular injuries share a rather explicit similarity to their genital referent."[4] This takes the gender ideals to extremes, forcing it into symbolism that half of the audience wouldn't recognize, and it isn't always the case. In *Psycho* and *Black Christmas*, respectively, the audience sees the expression on Marion's face or the crystal figure with blood on it, but they don't witness the actual murders. The audience doesn't see any of the characters get cut up in *Texas*, everything happens offscreen. Not one drop of blood is actually spilled in *Halloween* because they didn't have the budget for it. The most famous deaths in *Friday the 13th* are when Jack is stabbed from under the bed, which would be more phallic than gynocentric, and the ax in Marcie's face, which isn't removed for the audience to see the wound. Tina is sliced up by finger knives in *Nightmare*, but her body is being thrown around the room so the audience can't focus on the wounds. The deaths in *Scream* are disembowelments, throat slits (which are usually covered by the victim's hands), and being crushed in a garage door.

When these two authors talk about gender in slasher films, they look at it from the perspective that women are being picked on and killed just because they are women. What these notions fail to concede is that in most of these films, men die along with women. Most of the time, the gender barrier is broken down because the writer and director do something that had rarely been done before: they make a woman the hero. The portrayal of gender in these films can't and shouldn't be ignored because it is part of the rite of passage. The teens are trying to find their place in society, and they go through many exploratory phases until they find a comfortable space to operate in. The rite of passage gives them this chance because societal rules don't apply to them. Within the frame of the culture, strict gender regulations may be applied to the young individuals, but until they reaggregate themselves into society, they are free to explore the different ways to function across gender.

Clover and Dika try to classify the characters into either the category of masculine or feminine, but, unfortunately, they do not fit nicely into their respective stereotypes. Lila Crane seems to be an ideal female because she doesn't engage in premarital sex like her sister and she has to be rescued by Sam at the end of the film. However, she is unmarried, works outside the home, and continually pushes to get what she wants. She is not afraid to stand up to men and does it often.

All of the sorority girls are outside the traditional female stereotype. They drink, cuss, and have sex, and one of them is planning on having an abortion. They have no desire to become housewives and have a family. Jess appears to be a feminine character in both actions and appearance. She has long flowing hair and a quiet demeanor. She is concerned about the feelings of others, especially Clare when she thinks Barb is being mean to her. Then, the audience learns that she is pregnant and wants to get rid of the baby. She is calm and collected with her decision, and when she tells Peter, he freaks out. He is so emotional and upset about the ordeal, he completely blows his audition. Jess takes on a masculine role later in the film when

Peter meets her at the sorority house to make her change her mind. He tells her that he wants to get married and become a family, but Jess very calmly tells him that she doesn't want that kind of life and that she doesn't want to give up her dreams. He then begins to cry and begs her to reconsider. When she emotionlessly tells him no, he flees from the house.

At first, it seems like Sally is the template for feminine stereotypes: she swoons and passes out when confronted by danger, and when she is in the family's clutches, she tries to barter sexual favors for her life, and she screams and carries on when attacked. When it comes to Franklin, she takes on a very motherly role. She knows that he is afraid to be left alone in the dark, so to comfort him and make sure he is all right, she takes him with her over the rough terrain while she looks for her boyfriend. Of course, unlike a mother, she doesn't try to protect her brother when they are attacked. She runs away, screaming. Also uncharacteristic of female stereotypes, when she is given an opportunity to escape, she does. She realizes that her survival depends on her ability to get out of the house, and even though she injures herself in the process, she keeps going. If she had been a traditional female, she would have resigned herself to the inevitable and wound up like her friends.

Laurie has several stereotypical female traits. She is a good student, obeys her father when he asks her to do something, and can be trusted to babysit other people's children. She is a virgin and shy when it comes to boys. But, like Sally, she doesn't give up and let the killer have his way with her. On the contrary, she makes sure that the children are safe, then proceeds to defend herself. Although she gets injured in the process, she is still capable of defeating Michael.

Alice's traditional female attributes include her sensitive artistic side, her ability to clean cabins and pots and pans, and her virginity. She is afraid of snakes and needs help from a male to kill one in her room. However, she is also able to use a hammer and nails to fix a gutter. She is also strong enough to decapitate another human being with a machete.

Nancy in *Nightmare* is very motherly, and she stays the night at Tina's to make sure Tina feels safe. She visits Rod in jail to make sure he is all right and to get information. She turns down Glen's advances when he wants to make out. She even tucks her mother in when she is too drunk to do it herself. Like a typical female, she expects Glen and her father to save her. Unlike a typical female, she realizes the men might fail at their task of protecting her and reads survival guides and sets up booby traps to defeat Freddy.

As is expected of women, Sidney is very sensitive and cares about the feelings of those around her. Even though she didn't know the first victim very well, she still feels the loss while sitting in class. She is unwilling to have sex with Billy at first, but she undermines the stereotypical female traits by compromising and engaging in a make-out session and flashing her breasts. When she starts receiving threatening phone calls from the killer, she doesn't shy away in fear. She actually tries to call his bluff. This first instance occurs while she is at her house waiting for Tatum to pick her up. The killer calls and mentions he can see what she is doing. Instead of becoming upset and cowering in a corner, she steps onto the front porch and sticks her finger up her nose, taunting the person on the other end.

Clover argues that "the gender of the Final Girl is likewise compromised from the outset by her masculine interest, her inevitable sexual reluctance, her apartness from other girls, sometimes her name."[5] Yet it is exactly these things that allow her to overcome the killer. The whole purpose of the rite of passage is to turn societal rules upside down. As part of the rite of passage, each teen must become liminal, or in between, and flowing between masculine and feminine qualities does just that. The Final Girl survives because she can be both masculine and feminine, she is ambiguous. Many of the other characters are killed because they can't become completely ambiguous.

If the Final Girl is able to take care of herself, where does that leave the male characters or the female characters who get killed?

Dika explains that the sexual aggressiveness of the girls in *Halloween* is what makes them victims.[6] Her explanation centers on the fact that the females in the movie are sexual predators. They go after sex as is stereotypical of males in society: needing it all the time and not associating love with their desires. These girls mix both the masculine and feminine, but they do it in the wrong way. Laurie mixes the gender stereotypes in a way that is complementary to the notion of returning to the past. She respects the authority figures and takes responsibility for others. Lynda and Annie, on the other hand, are concerned with instant gratification and their selfish needs. They mock authority through their actions, and these attitudes are seen as going against cultural norms. If the girls had been like Laurie and were able to subdue their sexual desires, they would survive.

This would also explain why the sisters in the sorority house in *Black Christmas* are killed. Barb is very open about her sexuality and explains to Mr. Harrison how it takes three days for certain tortoises to mate. She compares that to zebras, who are finished rather quickly, much like her sexual encounters. She is crass and treats sex like a joke, which is evident at the police station when she gives the sergeant the sorority house's phone number. Unfortunately for the officer, he doesn't realize he is being toyed with and made fun of until later. Barb's aggressive/masculine notion of sexuality gets her killed in brutal fashion. But what about Clare? She doesn't engage in or talk about sex at all. Yet, she is the only character who kisses a boy onscreen and she has posters of naked people on her wall. She may not be as aggressive as Barb is when it comes to sex, but she is still interested in it, and that is socially unacceptable.

Marion also falls into the category of sexual aggressor because of her relationship with Sam. Granted, she wants to get married and be respectable, but when Sam tells her it's not feasible, she is willing to break up with him. It is possible she loves him, but when her desires are not met, she is willing to look elsewhere for gratification. This is also why she steals the money. She thinks she has found the quick fix to her dilemma. When she realizes it won't work, she decides to go back and make amends. Of course, it is too late; her aggressive attitude has already doomed her to death.

Tatum in *Scream* doesn't engage in sexual activity, but she is an aggressive female. Her manner of dress is sexually explicit even if she doesn't engage in sex onscreen. She wears tight shirts and shows off her midriff. She is constantly telling Dewey, her brother and a cop, to shut up and undermines his authority. When the killer confronts her in the garage, she fights back by throwing beer bottles at him and kicking him in the crotch. Unfortunately, this aggression doesn't save her, and she gets crushed by the garage door.

Even Casey, the first victim, has some aggressive tendencies. Before the conversation turns to threats, she flirts with the unknown caller, neglecting to mention her boyfriend and appearing available and willing to go on a date. When the caller freaks her out, she threatens him with her boyfriend, who is a football player and will kick his butt. When the killer attacks, she tries to protect herself and fight back. Sadly, it doesn't save her life.

Clover claims that boys die in these films because they make mistakes or go after "wrong" sex.[7] This notion doesn't make a lot of sense, because what is "right" sex? In terms of gender stereotypes, it is more acceptable for teenage males to be sexually promiscuous, but who are they going to have sex with? It would stand to reason that they would be interested in girls their own age, but female stereotypes dictate that teenage girls are supposed to remain virgins until they are married. In essence, the males in slasher films die for the same reason as females: because they are undermining cultural norms.

Clover and Dika make a big deal about the masculine traits of the Final Girl, but the rest of the characters are simply written off as feminine because of their passive reaction to the situation: "In their powerlessness they occupy a more 'feminine' position within the film, and, as devalued objects, they can be dispatched without regret."[8] The other characters may die without putting up much of a fight, but their role in the film goes beyond being just "devalued objects"; there is actually a purpose to their actions. The best examples of this can be seen when the characters are shown naked or scantily clad.

Most of the characters in these films are killed because of or when they are involved in some type of sexual activity. Marion Crane is murdered in the shower. She was not actively involved in any type of sexual activity, but Norman watched her undress and became aroused.

Lynda and Bob are murdered right after they have sex. Bob goes downstairs to get a beer out of the fridge, and Michael pins him to a door with a butcher knife. Afterward, Michael covers himself with a sheet, puts on Bob's glasses, and heads upstairs. Lynda is sitting on the bed filing her nails when the door opens. Thinking it's Bob, she begins to ask him questions and teases him with her bare breasts, but when he doesn't answer, she gets upset and turns to call Laurie. As she is about to speak, Michael comes up behind her and strangles her with the phone cord. Annie is killed in the car in the garage while getting ready to pick up her boyfriend. She hasn't engaged in sexual activity yet, but she is dressed in a shirt and panties with a coat and nothing else. She has every intention of having sex, but she never gets the chance.

For Jack and Marcie in *Friday the 13th*, the murders happen right after intercourse, and for Bill and Brenda, they were engaged in a rousing game of strip Monopoly and down to their underwear. Tina in *Nightmare* is also killed after engaging in sexual intercourse. She is attacked after rolling over to fall asleep. Rod is the second victim in the film, and even though his death doesn't occur right after sex, he was still involved in sexual activity. Glen wishes he could be involved in sexual practices, but he doesn't have a partner. He is killed after falling asleep while watching *Miss Nude America*.

The point here is that when it comes to sex in these films, there is no longer a blurring of the gender lines. The audience sees, as well as the characters, exactly who is male and who is female. There is no longer any ambiguity. When this blurring stops and the categories become socially distinct, such as during sex, the initiands fail the rite of passage, and, in the case of the film, they are killed.

Black Christmas, *Texas*, and *Scream* function differently than the other films because the characters don't engage in sexual activity onscreen. In *Texas*, they don't engage in sex at all. Instead of focusing on deviant sexual behavior, *Texas* focuses on the deviancy of being a nonproductive member of society. Pam and Kirk are killed when they venture onto the family's property in the hopes of bartering for gas. Jerry is killed when he goes to the house looking for Pam and Kirk. He notices the blanket the pair took with them, and proceeds inside. He finds Pam locked in a freezer, barely alive and convulsing, then he is killed by Leatherface with a sledgehammer. In both cases, the kids thought it was all right to enter someone else's property. Pam and Kirk did knock on the door, but when no one answered, they were drawn inside by what sounded like animal squeals. They have no sense of privacy or other people's property, so they are killed, in essence, for trespassing.

The other films have sexuality fused into them, and just because the characters don't engage in sex onscreen, that does not make them prudes when it comes to such activities. In *Black Christmas*, Clare is the only girl who kisses a boy. Even though they aren't having sex, that doesn't mean they won't in the future or that sexuality doesn't play a role. Barb talks about sex and alludes to the fact she has had it before. Jess is pregnant, so the audience knows she was sexually active. The only one who is a mystery is Phyl. She has a boyfriend, but the audience never sees them kiss and she doesn't talk about sex. There are some indications they are physically involved, but nothing concrete. After Barb gets off the phone with her mother and realizes she can't go home, she asks the other girls if they want to go on a ski trip. Both Jess and Phyl say yes. The next time we see Phyl's boyfriend, he is dressed up as Santa and upset because he won't be able to spend any time with Phyl. It's unclear if they were planning to have sex, but his attitude alludes to disappointment. Mrs. Mac's death is not due to sexual activity but just being in the wrong place at the wrong time. Even though the girls do not engage in sexual activity onscreen, they are still punished for the acts they engaged in previously or would engage in in the future.

Friday the 13th Part 2 reinforces many of these same traits through Ginny, the Final Girl, but this movie throws a twist into the teens' liminality: Ginny undresses onscreen and has sex with her boyfriend offscreen. Although the focus in the first film stressed that by engaging in sex or by showing off biological attributes, the characters void their liminality, this is not the case in this film; there is something else at play here. Remember, the purpose of the rites of passage and slasher films is to turn societal norms on their heads, which is exactly what this film does by altering the rules. It takes the basic premise from the first film and turns it around. This is done by making Ginny a nonvirgin and stronger than Alice in her ability to gaze back toward the killer. Ginny still has the same gender-based ambiguity as Alice, but she has a different freedom when it comes to sexuality and her place at this camp. While emphasis in the first film relied on ambiguity, the second one relies heavily on undermining social boundaries and regulations.

Again, the teens are in the transition phase, which means social definitions and rules don't apply to them. They have the freedom to explore their environment in whatever way they choose. In many cases, society has no repercussions against the teens' actions. This explains why the teens push the boundaries so far in these movies and why the killers punish them for their deeds.

This is especially evident when Jeff and Sandra decide to go explore the forbidden Camp Crystal Lake, which is right next to where they are staying. The two get caught by the local police and are taken to Paul, who is supposed to be in charge of the teens, for discipline. Much to the distaste of the officer, Paul only makes a joke that Jeff and Sandra's punishment will be not getting any dessert. The cop, who is the ultimate symbol of societal authority, has no other choice but to leave. To further emphasize the police officer's lack of power, he is murdered with the claw of a hammer.

Scream also relies on taking social norms and turning them upside down. Like Ginny, Sidney engages in sexual activity with her boyfriend (offscreen) yet is still able to defeat the killer. The other characters are not killed because of their sexual practices but because they are viewed as a way to torment Sidney. Slasher films had fallen out of popularity long before *Scream* was created. Audiences had grown weary of the same scenarios played out with slight variations. For *Scream* to resurrect the genre and gain popularity, it had to do away with old conventions. This was accomplished by the seemingly random murders. However, the basic premise hadn't changed: teens are still punished for engaging in behaviors outside of societal norms (basically for just being teens), and sexual activity plays a role in those actions. Even though the sexual action that motivates the killer comes from Sidney's mother, that doesn't mean the teens weren't capable of doing it. For example, Casey is planning on watching a movie with her boyfriend while her parents are gone. Does that mean they are going to have sex? Not necessarily, but the opportunity is there. The clothes Tatum wears throughout the entire film are very tight and sexually suggestive. Again, just because she doesn't engage in sex onscreen doesn't mean the opportunities aren't there. The film takes the audiences' expectations of what they think is going to happen and what has happened in earlier films and turns them on their heads.

Sex and sexuality places teens in a liminal stage, but so does their age. While the high school years are important in a teen's life, it is their college days that are the most informative. It places the teens outside of normal social boundaries and allows them freedom of exploration.

These institutions are a place that is set apart from normal society that allows teens to experiment with drugs, sex, and free thinking, under the assumption that, at the same time, they will go to classes and acquire the knowledge they will need to function as adults in the real world. In *Friday the 13th Part 2*, this explains why the teens are able to go into the bar in town. Granted, they don't do anything wrong or pillage the local townsfolk, but they are also not bothered. They are allowed to sit and discuss the story of Jason without any interruptions or adults chastising them for believing in silly legends. When Ted turns to one and asks him where the after party is, the adult doesn't even speak to him. During the transition phase, they are not part of normal society, but outside it, and this is restated at the end of the film when no one knows exactly what has happened to Paul or to Jason. The audience assumes that Paul is dead, but what happened to Jason? Why did he let Ginny go? If they were functioning in a normal social setting, the audience would get the answers that they desperately crave, but since the characters are outside of social norms, the audience is left to speculate about what really happened.

This also explains why the girls in *Black Christmas* get away with their behavior. As was mentioned earlier, expectations of teens at a university or college are different than expectations in the real world. They are allowed to freely explore and discover who they are as a person separate from their parents. As long as they continue to go to class and get good grades, the authority figures won't say anything about their extracurricular activities. This explains why the cops were so reluctant to search for Clare when she turned up missing. Since they function in an asocial environment, normal social rules don't apply to them. It was all right for Clare to run away and shack up with a boy because that action is accepted in the social context of being a college student.

The teens in these films who are able to function in this asocial way, the ones that break the social barriers, are the ones that survive. This can include engaging in sex or refraining from it. The implication is not that sex or sexuality in these films is bad. In many ways, it is just another aspect of asocial behavior. It is completely acceptable within the separate community of the teens. Sex, thus, plays a dual role in these films, and its other role ties into the purpose of the killer.

Don't Trust the Killers' Identity Crisis

Clover claims that the killer in these films is overtly masculine, most of the times to ridiculous extremes, even when the killer is a woman, as in the first *Friday the 13th*, but she also recognizes that many times the killer has ambiguous gender. However, she tries to sexualize the killer by turning the voyeuristic bouts into misplaced sexuality and the inability to fulfill his (or her) desires.[9] But this notion completely ignores the fact that most of these killers are out for revenge. The only killer who engages in voyeuristic tendencies is Norman. When he is sexually aroused, his mother's personality takes over and kills the object of desire out of jealousy. These feelings stem from Norman's sense of abandonment when his mother left him for her lover. The killer in *Black Christmas* doesn't watch any of the girls undress or engage in any type of sexual activity. He kills them whenever the opportunity suits him best. In *Texas*, the family has been displaced by technology and has to do what they can to survive. The sex that occurs in *Halloween* and *Friday the 13th* only reinforces the killers' anger, not because they are unable to have it but because it was the cause of the horrific event that led to their murdering spree. Freddy's focus is on revenge and he targets the kids whose parents killed him. Billy wants to make Sidney pay for actions committed by her mother. He has sex with Sidney, so his desires are taken care of, but none of the other victims in the film engages in the activity.

At first glance, these killers do appear to be overtly masculine, but they all have both masculine and feminine traits. Norman dresses in his mother's clothes to kill and has incorporated her personality into his. The killer in *Black Christmas* speaks in a woman's voice on the phone after murdering the girls. Hitchhiker has long hair and a slender build. Leatherface dons a female mask and dress while preparing dinner for the family. Cook is so named because of his inability to kill and the desire to perform a task that is normally done by women. The desires of the men from *Texas* are also largely unknown. It is evident there are no women around for them to engage in sexual intercourse with, but when they kidnap Sally, they have no intention of using her for their sexual desires. Even when she offers them sexual favors to let her go, they have no idea what she is talking about.

In *Halloween*, the audience never really knows why Michael goes after his sister, but he murders her right after she engages in sex with her boyfriend. The majority of the subsequent murders happen after the teens have had sex or are about to have sex. Michael is also portrayed as being an incredibly masculine character, but like the other characters in the film, he has moments of ambiguity. For example, the first time he committed murder was when he was a child. It is hard to imagine that he would have had overtly masculine traits at ten, especially when he hadn't even reached his sexual peak. Afterward, he was locked in an asylum away from the influences of society and the pressures that would have come with gender stereotypes. Throughout the majority of the film, he also wears a nondescript mask.

Mrs. Voorhees is even portrayed as being incredibly masculine. The small bits of her the audience sees are heavy work boots and plaid shirts, which are used as a construct of the director to make the audience believe the killer is male. She also seems to have incredible strength and can hurl Brenda's body through a window. But by the end of the film, it is very apparent the killer is female.

Freddy in *Nightmare* is thin and sharpens his finger knives the way women file their nails. Unlike Michael, he doesn't wear a mask, but his face has been so badly burned it's almost unrecognizable. The costume the killers wear in *Scream* is very dress-like and they also cover their faces with a mask. When Billy is not in costume, his hair is constantly in his face, he has very soft facial features, and he tries to be sensitive to Sidney's feelings and needs. This is especially evident when the kids are at school after the first murder. They are sitting on a bench talking about what happened, and Stuart makes comments that upset Sidney. Billy keeps telling him to be quiet, but he doesn't stop, so Sidney eventually gets up and leaves. Unlike other boys his age (including Billy), Stuart doesn't seem to be obsessed with sex. He has a girlfriend, but they don't engage in any risky behaviors. They are barely seen kissing onscreen.

Like the teens, the killers have to be able to function in a liminal way. By combining the different gender types, they become just as ambiguous as the teens. However, the masculine part of each of the killers overrides the feminine throughout the course of the films, and this is how the Final Girl is able to defeat them. Once the killer loses the ability to blend both masculine and feminine traits, they lose the power of ambiguity and can be defeated.

Be Unpredictable

Part of the process in a rite of passage is taking normal social expectations and turning them on their heads. This happens often in slasher films because the teens operate outside of normal social boundaries, but also because the killers create their own idealized past and notions of how the teens are supposed to act within those ideals. Defamiliarizing normal social expectations also puts the audience on the edge of their seats. It creates fear because the audience doesn't know what is going to happen.

This defamiliarization of the normal is rampant throughout all the films and can be seen from the opening sequence. *Psycho* begins with a shot of Phoenix, then takes the audience into a hotel room where they meet Sam and Marion after a sexual tryst. The expectation the film sets up is that it is a normal city on a normal day, but that is quickly dispelled when the audience learns about the socially unacceptable relationship between the characters. At first, it seems like they are happy together, but then the tension builds and they argue about respectability and getting married. It becomes obvious Marion is desperate, even though she tries to play it cool, which is why she steals the money. The normal reaction to her crime is for her to flee, which she does. Her attempt to get to Sam with the money is tense and full of moments when it's possible Marion could get caught, but she doesn't; she makes it to the Bates Motel, only fifteen miles away from Sam. The expectation this part of the film sets up is that Marion and Sam will live happily ever after, but then she has second thoughts about what she's done. The film is defamiliarized when she is stabbed to death in the shower.

The beginning of *Black Christmas* shows the outside of the sorority house decorated with lights while carols are playing. The audience watches as Barb enters the house and joins the others at the party. It then switches to first-person perspective of some unknown character who watches the group from the window, then sneaks around to the side of the house and climbs into the attic. The film sets up the expectation that the girls are enjoying the holidays, but the audience knows something bad is going to happen when the unknown individual sneaks into the house. The tranquility and joy of Christmas is quickly replaced with dread and death. This is further emphasized with the obscene phone call. As the party winds down, Jess answers the phone and hears heavy breathing. She calls to the others, who all gather around to listen. Barb takes the phone and starts to taunt the caller before he threatens to kill her and hangs up. The only person who seems to be truly upset about the whole situation is Clare. The other girls shrug it off and go about their business. The audience goes upstairs with Clare and expects to watch her pack and get ready to leave, but then those expectations are shattered when she is suffocated with a clothes bag. Even the killer gets caught in defamiliarization. His actions have been to climb down from the attic at his own will to murder his next victim, but Mrs. Mac discovers his hiding place and Clare's body. He kills her but is then thrown into a fit of rage because the death wasn't according to his plan. From that point on, the audience doesn't know when or who the killer will strike next.

In *Texas*, the film starts out with scrolling text that explains how Sally and Franklin were attacked. The expectation it sets up is that the film is based on actual events, that it's a documentary, but then it fades to black and the sound of digging can be heard. Light flashes to reveal body parts, and a radio announcer reports on the recent grave robberies occurring in Texas. The camera centers on the half-rotted face of a corpse then pans out to show a grisly display that is wired to a headstone. The announcer explains that multiple grave robberies have occurred, and a dozen empty crypts have been found. He says that in most cases, only parts of the bodies, not the entire corpse, have been taken, and the police have no suspects in custody. He claims that dozens of families have converged on the cemetery to make sure their relatives' graves have been undisturbed.

The audience knows something terrible is going to happen to Sally and Franklin—the text at the beginning of the film told them that—but they don't know what. The film sets itself up as a familiar horror story by claiming to be based on true events, but then it defamiliarizes itself by opening with a tale of grave robberies. What do grave robbers have to do with Sally and Franklin? They learn shortly after that the trip they are on is to find out if their family plots have been disturbed, but the image of the corpses on the headstone takes the audience out of the familiar and places them into the realm of death and the macabre. After the title, the camera focuses on a dead armadillo with the van as a fuzzy shape in the background. It pulls over on the side of the road, and a male gets out, pulling wooden ramps out of the side door. He disappears into the van and reemerges a few minutes later with another male in a wheelchair, whom the first male pushes into the weeds and hands a can. The audience recognizes the individual has to pee, but for many, it would be an unfamiliar task since they probably aren't confined to a wheelchair. As he is performing his duty, a semi drives by on the highway, honking his horn and startling the men. The one in the wheelchair rolls down a hill, through tall bushes, and is then spilled onto the ground. A girl pokes her head out of the passenger side window and yells, "Franklin!" From this moment on, the audience is out of familiar territory. They may be able to relate to the hippie interest in the alignment of the planets, but they more than likely have no idea what it is like to travel with an invalid. The landscape itself is defamiliarized through death and drought.

Halloween begins with a first-person camera shot of an unknown individual looking through the window at a teenage girl and her boyfriend. When the boyfriend asks if they are alone, the girl responds that Michael is around somewhere, but the audience doesn't know who Michael is or what relationship he might have with the two inside. They go upstairs to have sex, and the person who was watching walks into the kitchen and grabs a butcher knife from the drawer. The audience now realizes that this person, whoever it may be, is the killer. Still in first-person camera, the killer heads upstairs, along the way putting on a mask, which condenses the field of vision into two peepholes. The audience sees the girl who had been downstairs sitting at the vanity, brushing her hair. The killer approaches her, then begins to stab her over and over with the knife. When finished, the killer goes downstairs and out the front door, running into an adult, who removes the mask to reveal a young boy.

The film sets up the expectation that something bad is going to happen. When the audience sees the figure grab the knife, they are pretty sure someone is going to die. The expectations are defamiliarized when the audience finds out that a child has committed the murder. Defamiliarization also occurs when Michael puts on his mask. Although Halloween is a time when people are allowed to run around in disguises, they normally don't kill people. The normality of a holiday is defamiliarized through the brutal murders Michael enacts. The once calm, quiet suburb is transformed into an unfamiliar hunting ground. The notion that he comes from an asylum also places him outside of society. His thoughts and actions are well outside of normal social boundaries.

Like *Halloween*, the opening sequence of *Friday the 13th* shows us a first-person perspective. The film begins with someone in the woods, and the audience can hear teens singing in the background. We walk with the unidentified person as the person makes his or her way through a cabin to check on the children. The camera switches out of first person and focuses on teens around a campfire. As they sing religious songs, two teens make googly eyes at one another then get up and walk off hand in hand. They go into a barn and climb to the loft where they start kissing. The camera switches back into first person, and the audience slowly creeps upstairs with the unknown individual. As the person approaches the teens, a floorboard creaks, alerting the teens that they are not alone. They both jump up and come face-to-face with the unknown person. It is obvious the boy knows who this person is because he immediately launches into an explanation that they weren't doing anything. The unknown person proceeds to stab the boy, and the girl becomes hysterical. Cornered, she paces back and forth and pleads for her life. The murderer approaches her slowly, and the last frame before the title is the girl frozen in a silent scream.

The expectation this film sets up is that the camp is full of good, wholesome individuals. The unknown person is concerned with the well-being of the children, which is why he or she checks on them in their beds, and the counselors are singing religious songs around a campfire. These expectations are defamiliarized when the teens run off to find a private place to have sex and the unknown individual kills them for their misdeeds. The normal reaction would have been for the teens to get into trouble, perhaps be verbally chastised for what they did. The teens believe they will get into some trouble, hence the boy's quick explanation of what they were doing and the girl's reaction when he gets killed.

Friday the 13th Part 2 begins with a little kid splashing in puddles and singing. His mother calls him from the house and tells him to come inside, which he does reluctantly, and the camera switches to first person. Again, the audience does not know who the person is, but the person gazes at a house for a while before approaching it. The camera then switches out of first person and shows us Alice asleep on her bed, twitching from a nightmare. We delve into her subconscious and see she is dreaming about the final confrontation on the banks of Crystal Lake. The entire end of the film is replayed before Annie wakes up in a panic. She decides she is going to take a shower, and the camera pans out of the room. The audience sees her throw her clothes onto the bed, and she walks across the hall to the bathroom in her robe. Alice senses something isn't right, and constantly keeps looking over her shoulder. She climbs into the bathtub and pulls the curtain shut, and the view seems to have switched back into first person. As it slowly approaches the shower, Alice quickly flings open the curtain to find no one there. Her phone rings, and she steps out to answer it. She talks to her mother for a while then hangs up. The phone rings again, but no one is there. The creepy feeling returns, and Alice steps into her living room. She locks her door then notices the window is open. A sound from the kitchen draws her attention, and she heads in. When she realizes it was only the cat, she asks it if it's hungry. She puts on a kettle then turns to the fridge. When she opens it, she notices the decapitated head of Mrs. Voorhees and screams. Someone grabs her from behind and stabs an ice pick into her temple. The final scene before the credits is the unknown assailant removing the whistling kettle, which sounds eerily similar to Alice's scream, from the burner.

The expectation the film sets up is that the audience will be able to see how Alice has reintegrated into society. It defamiliarizes this expectation by showing that Alice has not made it back to society at all. In the conversation with her mother on the phone, Alice specifically says the only way she knows how to get her life back is to be alone. Irritated, she then tells her mother she will talk to her tomorrow and hangs up. The film also defamiliarizes the expectations of the audience because Alice is the first person in the film to die. She was lucky enough to survive the encounter with Mrs. Voorhees, but this new killer takes her by surprise and kills her without ceremony. Whatever power Alice had at Camp Crystal Lake is lost when she returns to the "real world."

The beginning of *Nightmare* shows an unknown person collecting knives and affixing them onto a glove. He then sharpens them with care and slides the glove onto his hand. After the credits, the scene switches to show the knives cut through a canvas, then we see Tina running down a dark, wet hallway. It is obvious that someone

Freddy (Robert Englund) surprises Tina (Amanda Wyss) in *A Nightmare on Elm Street* (1984). *New Line Cinema/Photofest* © *New Line Cinema*

is chasing her because she keeps looking over her shoulder. Oddly, a sheep startles her, and she heads into a boiler room. The man with the knives comes after her, and Tina runs for her life, turning down a hallway, which turns out to be a dead end. She sees the shadow of the man and screams. Both she and the audience expect the man to come after her, but he doesn't. She takes a few steps to head out, and the man pops up behind her, jerking her out of sleep.

The film sets up the expectation that people are going to get hurt or killed by the knife glove, but it defamiliarizes those expectations by taking the audience into the world of dreams. Nightmares are not a new occurrence, and more than likely everyone in the audience has probably experienced one, so they can relate to the fear on that level. Things become unfamiliar when the nightmare actually kills the teens.

Scream begins with a young girl getting ready to watch a movie. The phone rings, and she answers. When she doesn't recognize the voice on the other end, she tells him that he has the wrong number and gets ready to hang up. He convinces her not to, and a conversation ensues. They talk about her plans for the evening, which include watching a scary movie with her boyfriend, and they discuss horror movies. Things get creepy when the person on the other end of the line asks for the girl's name, saying he wants to know whom he's looking at. Things really take a turn for the worse when she discovers her boyfriend has been tied up on the back porch and is then disemboweled. The killer goes after the girl, who tries to flee for her life. It looks as if she will get help because her parents come home and she is only steps away from them. Unfortunately, she can't scream because she has been hit in the throat. Her parents hear her on the phone, and since they can't use it to call the police, the father sends the mother to the neighbors to call. When she steps onto the porch, she discovers her daughter's body hanging from a tree and screams. The credits roll.

Scream sets up the expectations that the teens are going to be killed like all the other teens in previous slasher films. It does this by referencing earlier films, but then it defamiliarizes the expectations by throwing in the sense of hope. As Casey is being chased by the killer, there is the sense the parents will save her. This, of course, is quickly dispelled. Even the actions of the Final Girl are different from those before her. In previous films, the Final Girl was never aware of the killer until she finds her friends' bodies. In this film, she is very aware of the murders, but instead of shying away, which is typical of the character until she is cornered, she immediately challenges the killer. The stereotypes of the genre are also defamiliarized by making the killers teens and by having two of them. The film also has more than one survivor at the end help defeat the killer.

The use of first-person camera also defamiliarizes the settings of these films because it forces the audience to relate to the killer. In traditional horror films, the audience is kept separate from the bad guy; they are usually portrayed as being from outside of society and a menace to the normal way of life. They must be defeated and conquered. In slasher films, the killer is, or at one time was, a part of society. Their actions are driven by the perceived wrongs that society imposed on them or by the change the teens are trying to enact. By forcing the audience into their perspective, it shows just how destructive and unfamiliar society has become.

These films also defamiliarize the killers by giving them supernatural qualities. Each one of them seems to have superhuman strength and each one of them seems to be indestructible. Norman is able to knock Sam out near the end of the film despite being smaller. The killer in *Black Christmas* is able to drag Clare's body up the ladder to the attic with no one hearing and, seemingly, without any issues. It's possible she is incredibly light, but he still has to carry her over his shoulder and make it through the attic door quietly. Then, when Mrs. Mac comes into the attic to find the cat, he skewers her with a hook and pulley. Being able to throw the hook hard enough to actually pierce the skin would be lucky. More than likely, he would have just knocked her in the head and she would have fallen down the ladder, but his shot actually gets the hook under her chin and kills her so he can hoist her up.

Leatherface has the ability to kill teen boys with one blow to the head with a sledgehammer and can hang a girl on a hook without breaking a sweat. Granted, he would have performed the same task in a slaughterhouse where a cow's skull is thicker than a human's, but he is also working in a controlled environment. It was pretty much luck that Kirk happened to be in the right place and didn't flinch when Leatherface raised the hammer over his head. At the end of the film, Leatherface slices himself with his own chain saw, yet still has the ability to chase Sally down the road.

The opening sequence of *Halloween* shows a young boy murdering his sister. Although he surprises her when he enters the room, she still would have been able to fight him off if she had tried. Michael is half his sister's size, yet he still has the ability to stab her repeatedly. At the end of the film, even though he has been stabbed with a knitting needle, poked in the eye with a hanger, shot, and has fallen out of a two-story window, he still disappears into the night. But it's not only his ability to survive that makes him supernatural. Phillips points out that Michael seems to influence the events. He claims these are most evident in the scene with Annie in the laundry room and when Laurie finds all of her friends dead.[10] None of the other characters seem to realize Michael is influencing both their lives and deaths. They don't attribute any supernatural powers to him, but Dr. Loomis claims that Michael is pure evil.

Jason from *Friday the 13th Part 2* and subsequent films functions in much the same way as Leatherface and Michael. Supposedly, he drowned when he was a child, but the second film finds him living in a shack in the woods. How he has survived without being detected and how he has grown up to possess superhuman strength is a mystery. Like the other two characters, Jason is not easily killed. He can sustain a lot of injury, be cut on the leg with his own machete, yet he still has the ability to get up and continue his pursuit of his victims. Like Michael, Jason has the ability to set bodies up in a way that makes them pop out at the right moment when the Final Girl comes looking for them. As the series continues, Jason becomes unnaturally strong. In part 9, his physical body is no longer present, yet his spirit has the ability to possess people and make them do his will.

Freddy is pretty much completely supernatural because he was burned to death in a fire and can only exist in dreams. He can only attack his victims when they are asleep, but his influence reaches into the real world. Since no one can fight sleep forever, he just waits patiently for them. However, once he is in the real world, he can supposedly be vanquished. Nancy believes that she defeats him by turning her back on him. He lunges at her and disappears without a trace. But the next scene shows that he might not be defeated that easily. As Nancy climbs into the car with her friends, the top of the convertible closes, looking a lot like Freddy's sweater, and then all the doors lock. The teens are trapped inside as it drives down the street. Nancy's mother seems oblivious to what is going on and waves from the front porch. In the final scene, the window of the door breaks and the knife-gloved hand of Freddy pulls Marge through.

Mrs. Voorhees functions slightly different than the other killers because she is killed at the end of the film. However, she does have the supernatural ability of strength. The bodies of dead teens are thrown through windows and stuck to doors with arrows, a feat that could only be accomplished by someone with a lot of strength, not necessarily a middle-aged woman. Her supernatural strength becomes even more evident when she gets into a fight with Alice. For someone who can throw a body through a window, Mrs. Voorhees has issues subduing her last victim; she is beat down and knocked out, but she always gets back up. Mrs. Voorhees's supernatural influence also comes into play during the numerous attempts to reopen the camp, which were thwarted by mysterious fires and poisoned water. No one seems to believe that a person could have been doing all those things to the camp; instead, they claim that the camp is cursed and haunted.

The killers in *Scream* are a lot like Mrs. Voorhees and are killed at the end of the film. For sure Billy is killed, but the audience really never knows what happens to Stuart, though it is assumed he dies because the last time we see him, he collapses from his stab wounds. Before we know that there are two killers, there is a supernatural quality to him because he seems to be everywhere at once.

The killers' supernatural powers allows them to return throughout the course of the series. However, despite this influence, they can still be defeated. They just don't stay down for long.

How to Survive

Part of the process in the rite of passage is learning how to function as an adult in society, and that means learning how to work. After all, as an adult, you are defined by what you do and how well you can provide. Most teens have an aversion to work, so the skills have to be taught in a way that is acceptable to teens. If they believe they are playing as they are being taught job skills, the teens may be more apt to learn. By being able to combine work with play, society is able to teach teens how they are supposed to act within the adult world without making it seem like a tedious ordeal. Laurie is the best example of work mixed with play. The most obvious example is her babysitting responsibilities. Here, she is in charge of taking care of Tommy, but it's not all business; she is allowed to laugh and have fun. As a representative of the liminal group, Laurie is caught between the young generation and the adult generation. As a babysitter, she has to be a responsible adult, but she is also allowed to be childlike. She mixes both of these qualities well until she is attacked by Michael.

Alice from *Friday the 13th* is also a good example of how to mix work and play. The first time the audience meets her, she is coming out of a cabin carrying a bucket and sponge. Steve, the camp's owner, is speaking to the other teens, who have just driven up in a truck and helped him pull a tree stump out. Alice explains that she has finished cleaning the cabin, and Steve instructs her to get the others started working. Ned complains that they have two weeks and reluctantly follows to start his chores. The next scene with Alice shows her nailing a gutter back onto the roof of a cabin. Steve comes over to talk to her, commenting on her handy abilities, then notices her sketch book. He picks it up and glances at the pictures, telling Alice that she has a lot of talent. When he finds a picture of himself, presumably looking a little angry, he asks her if that is how he always looks. She responds by telling him that he looked like that the previous night. The implication here is that while she spends all day helping Steve get the camp ready, she spends the evenings relaxing and drawing in her book.

A little while later, Steve leaves to get supplies in town. Almost immediately, the teens dress in their bathing suits and head down to the lake. They spend some time swimming and bathing in the sun then eventually head back to work. Alice lounges on the beach with the others but then seems to be the only one who actually goes back to work. After a run-in with a snake in her room (in which all the teens offer their assistance even though she only asked Bill to help her), while Ned is running around the camp with a feathered headdress on his head and his shirt tied like a diaper, Alice is in the kitchen cleaning pots and pans. When the storm finally hits and the teens are forced indoors, Alice, Bill, and Brenda sit in the main cabin and play strip Monopoly until Brenda remembers that she left her window open and leaves to close it. Alice soon finds herself alone as the other teens are murdered.

Like Laurie, Alice's ability to mix play and work places her in a liminal place between the adult world and the teen world. She knows how to take care of her responsibilities, yet she still takes the time to have fun with her friends. The other teens do some chores around the camp, but they are not nearly as hardworking as Alice or as dedicated to their jobs.

The girls in *Black Christmas* also know how to mix work and play. While they are at school, they are expected to attend classes and get good grades. But they also have the freedom to drink, hang out with boys, and have sex. Unfortunately, they don't mix their responsibilities well because all of them are murdered.

Sally is slightly different from the others because her responsibility for her brother comes out of obligation. Initially, the teens venture out to make sure that Sally and Franklin's family graves haven't been disturbed, but then they decide to go to the old house to check it out. The group consists of Sally and her boyfriend and Pam and Kirk, who are also in a relationship. Franklin is the fifth wheel because he isn't involved with anyone. Sally is extremely concerned for her brother when the van pulls onto the side of the road so Franklin can go to the bathroom and he rolls down the hill and is tossed out of his chair. But she doesn't seem to be as concerned when they make it to the family house. He is unable to maneuver through the crumbling ruins, but that doesn't stop Sally and the others from touring the house and having fun. Later, when Sally and Franklin are waiting for the others to come back to the van, Franklin tries to engage his sister in conversation, but it is obvious she isn't interested. When Franklin is scared, such as when she wants to leave to find her boyfriend and he doesn't want to be left alone at the van, despite the physical limitations, she takes him with her. Sally has the ability to balance her concern for her brother and still have her own life.

Nancy takes on a very motherly role and takes responsibility for making sure Tina feels safe after her nightmare. Even when Tina's boyfriend shows up and they leave to have sex, Nancy doesn't leave because Tina asks her to stay. She doesn't even give in to make out with Glen because of her obligations to her friend. Even after Tina's death, Nancy continues to go to school and tries to maintain a normal life. She doesn't seem to have much play in her life because she is constantly taking care of others, even her mother. She has moments of childlike behaviors—when her mother tells her she has a glass of warm milk and Nancy thinks that's gross, her hope that her father will save her, and asking for help from her boyfriend.

When that fails, she has to rely on herself, and all notions of fun and play become nonexistent. This explains why she is unable to defeat Freddy; she has no balance between work and play.

In *Scream*, Sidney tries to act like her other friends. However, she is still recovering from the murder of her mother, and her father is always traveling, so she is forced to rely on herself. She goes to parties, but she doesn't have fun while there. She has a boyfriend, but she doesn't seem to enjoy being touched by him. Eventually, she decides to give into the play side and has sex with Billy. Her ability to let go of her sadness and misery for a brief moment is enough to counter her constant seriousness and ensure her survival.

Marion seems to be the opposite of the teens—she is constantly working. She has a full-time job at a real estate agency. But, she doesn't take her position seriously. She is late getting back from lunch because she was having sex with Sam. She was just lucky her boss wasn't back. Then, she has to leave early because she has a headache. Her boss says she can leave as long as she takes the money to the bank, but she absconds with it instead. Even when she is supposed to be having fun, when she is with Sam, all she can think about is marriage and respectability. An enjoyable afternoon of sex gets tainted with anger and hurt feelings. Again, the inability for this character to mix work and play is what gets her killed.

The teens in these movies who are murdered are the ones who don't have a balance of work and play. They work when they have to, but they don't take responsibility like the Final Girls. The teens in *Texas* are a great example of how without the balance of work and play, they are just lambs for the slaughter. As representatives of the hippie generation, it is safe to assume that none of the teens in the film work or go to school. They are the extreme representatives of play, and the killers in the films are the extreme representations of work. In the context of the film, there needs to be a nice balance between work and play if the teens expect to return to society.

This notion of work and play ties back into the many uses of sex in the films. The teens represent the fun side of sex because they engage in it for gratification. The adults represent the work side of sex because they have children to take care of. This definition of sex ties into the ideals of ritual and liminality much in the same way as gender and magic functions in these films: it allows the teens a freedom to explore themselves and others without fear of repercussions. While they are outside of society, they are allowed to engage in sexual activity as the individual sees fit, knowing that when they rejoin the culture, this freedom of sexual play will have to stop. Social expectations dictate that they will give up their wild ways, settle down, and use sex only as a tool for populating the community. This is not to say that pregnancy doesn't happen in the teens group; it does, and it is not highly looked upon by the greater society.

All the films in the series have some type of sex or sexuality fused into them; it is part of the slasher film formula. Sex is incorporated into these films to further separate the teens from adult society or, in the case of Marion, to just separate her from society. The sex between the teens is very carefree and fun.

The teen community is set up to be the fun and explorative side of sex with the situations being very laid back and lighthearted. On the other side of this, the adult community is set up to be the work side of sex. Here, the situations become grotesque and uneasy. In the beginning, Sam and Marion probably enjoyed one another's company, but when the film opens, there is tension because Marion wants to get married. Norman has twisted the idea of sex and desire into jealousy and murder. When his mother abandoned him to be with her lover, he became insanely jealous and killed them. To fill the void of his mother's loss, he incorporates her personality into his and believes she would be just as jealous if he sexually desired another woman. Hence his need to dress as a woman and kill females who sexually arouse him.

This is especially evident in *Texas* where there are no females to have sex with. Even after the family captures Sally, they don't view her as a sex object. When she offers to do anything to save her life, the men mock and laugh at her. The situation is grotesque because the natural order of things has been disrupted. Unlike Grandpa's generation, who had children to pass on the family name and work skills, the next generation of males has no reason to have progeny to pass their skills to. Grandpa was the first generation to work in the slaughterhouse, and he had every intention of passing his skills down, which is evidenced in the fact that Hitchhiker used to work there also. When Grandpa lost his job to a machine, the family fell apart. Without a skill set to pass to the next generation, there is no need to have children, and the older generation becomes obsolete.

Jess and Peter in *Black Christmas* seem to have a great relationship until the pregnancy occurs. Jess decides that she doesn't want the responsibility and doesn't want to give up her dreams. Peter wants to have the child and get married. Their relationship becomes uneasy and they start to fight. Jess takes on a cold persona and tries to shut Peter out of her life, while he turns into an emotional wreck and threatens her. The relationship reaches grotesque levels when Jess beats Peter to death with a fireplace poker.

Mrs. Mac, who is supposed to be the housemother, is a grotesque representation of the adult world. Her job, like any parent, is to ensure that the girls get a good education and are morally sound. Unfortunately, that is too much to ask of Mrs. Mac. Her only real concern is finding another bottle of liquor. Mr. Harrison, as a father figure, is also a grotesque representation. He comes to the college to pick up Clare, and when she doesn't show up at the meeting place, he goes to the house to find her. When she still can't be found, they go to the police station. Mr. Harrison, like any parent, is concerned about his daughter, but he doesn't seem to be too concerned. At the police station, he doesn't get angry and demand they look for his daughter; that task is left to Chris. He still has plenty of time to eat and be waited on at the sorority house, instead of looking for his daughter; and at the end of the film, he faints and has to be taken care of.

In *Halloween*, like *Texas*, there aren't many adult women around for the men to have sex with. The nurse is one of the few, but it is very apparent that her and Dr. Loomis's relationship is strictly professional. The only time you see a mother in the film is at the beginning when Michael's parents return home after the murder of his sister and when Annie is entering the house she is supposed to babysit at. Otherwise, adult females are nonexistent in the film. Aside from the lack of women, the reason the men never have time for sex is because they are always working. The first and only time we see Laurie's father, he is carrying his briefcase, getting ready to go to work. In fact, her father is so busy he doesn't have time to drop off the key at the Myers house. Dr. Loomis and Mr. Brackett, the sheriff, are hunting down a maniacal killer.

Dr. Loomis's entire existence is focused on ensuring that Michael never gets out of the asylum. When he does escape, Dr. Loomis can't rest until he is found. When he and the nurse first pull up to the asylum, they notice some of the patients milling around the grounds in the pouring rain. The nurse wonders if they should call someone, but Dr. Loomis wants to find out if Michael is still there. While he is at the gate, talking on the phone, Michael attacks the nurse in the car. She eventually gets away, jumping out of the car and almost rolling into a ditch. Dr. Loomis is so focused on his task and so upset that Michael got away, he doesn't even check to see if the nurse is all right.

As sheriff, Mr. Brackett is always busy taking care of crime in Haddonfield, even though it doesn't seem like too much goes on. The first time the audience meets him is right after Annie goes into her house and Laurie is busy looking for the man who hid behind the bushes. Since she's not paying attention to what's in front of her, she runs into Mr. Brackett, who is heading into his house in the middle of the afternoon. The next time he is onscreen, he is checking out a robbery that occurred at the local hardware store. After that, Dr. Loomis convinces him to help him look for Michael. Their world is one that revolves around work, leaving no time for play.

Mrs. Voorhees has created a child, which is the ultimate expression of sex as work. But when she loses him, she loses her mind. The

Dr. Loomis (Donald Pleasance) is serious and determined to find Michael in *Halloween*.
Universal Pictures/Photofest © Universal Pictures; Photographer: Kim Gottlieb

situation becomes grotesque when Alice and the audience learn that Jason was deformed as a child. Mrs. Voorhees comments to Alice that Jason was a special child, one that needed to be watched all the time, especially because he wasn't a good swimmer. He drowned because the counselors were busy making love, but it makes one wonder where his mother was at the time. If Jason had such special needs and needed constant supervision, why didn't Mrs. Voorhees supply it to him?

Some of the adults in *Nightmare* still have fun with sex, such as Tina's mother, but the relationship is uneasy because the boyfriend seems bothered by Tina's presence. Her mother is torn between needing to be there for her daughter or taking care of her own needs. Her own needs win out, and she leaves for Vegas. Nancy's parents are divorced, and they can barely remain civil to one another. The relationship is uneasy because there is always the underlying tension that they could burst into an argument at any moment. All the relationships with the parents become grotesque when they fail to do their most important task: protect their kids.

Again, in *Scream*, parents are largely absent. The relationships are uneasy because they have been torn apart by affairs and murder. Several families have been destroyed by and children have been abandoned because of the parents' indiscretion. The relationships become grotesque when Billy feels he needs to murder people in the hopes of making Sidney pay and having his mother return.

The importance these situations have in the films is to set up a binary between the adult world and the teens' world, reinforcing how separate the teens are from normal society. These situations relate to the work side of sex because the parents have the responsibility of taking care of the product that was the result of earlier intercourse: their kids. They are fully functioning in a society that demands they teach their teens how to act appropriately, and this, in the context of the films, means that sex is no longer fun. Most of the time, the adults don't even have a partner around that they could have sex with. The parents' only important task is to make sure their teens make it to be adults.

Within the context of slasher films, the normal ideals and stereotypes of the nuclear family are broken down and dismantled. The teens are supposed to be functioning in a world outside of the normal, but they are supposed to be learning skills that will allow them to become adults. Unfortunately, most of the teens don't survive to return to the adult world, and even the adults can't function properly. These films show how the system has failed.

Mrs. Mac in *Black Christmas* is supposed to supervise the sorority girls, but her only concern is finding her next drink. The police believe Clare has run off and shacked up with some guy, and when another mother comes to the station to report her daughter missing, they don't take the mother seriously. At first, Lt. Fuller seems like he is just going to ignore it, asking if it's really out of the ordinary for the woman's daughter to be late. Even when she says that it is, he still doesn't seem too concerned. Again, it is only when Chris intervenes that anything gets done. Even though the teens are supposed to be in a liminal stage, that doesn't give the police or adults the right to completely disregard their duties.

In *Halloween*, there are hardly any parents around. Again, this shows how separate the teens are from the adult world. In one scene, Annie picks Laurie up so they can head to their babysitting jobs, and Annie hands Laurie a joint when she enters the car. They talk about various things, then notice Annie's father, the sheriff, in front of a store. Annie tells Laurie to get rid of the joint, and they stop to talk to Mr. Brackett. When they get back in, Laurie is concerned he knew about the marijuana, but Annie tells her not to worry about it. Mr. Brackett is in an odd situation if he did know the girls were smoking pot. On one hand, as a police officer, he would have to do his job and bust them for possession of an illegal drug. On the other hand, as a father, he should punish his child for breaking the law. But within the context of the films, the teens are allowed to function within their own space. They know what they are doing is wrong, but they also know they will not get into trouble for doing it. They are liminal, and, therefore, allowed to explore their world freely.

In *Friday the 13th*, the grotesque side of the adult world becomes evident when Annie enters the local diner to ask directions to Camp Crystal Lake. The waitress in the diner has so much makeup on she looks almost clown-like, another woman is dressed as if she just walked out of the fifties, and the man who offers to give her a ride

looks like he hasn't bathed recently. He also takes advantage of Annie as she is climbing into the truck and gropes her butt. There is
also Ralph, the local crazy who warns the teens they are all doomed,
who is unshaven and spouts off random warnings. Even the police
officer who comes to camp seems to be ineffectual. He tries to portray an air of authority, but he actually ends up looking like a joke
to the teens.

The adults in *Nightmare* are actually the ones who doom their
children. When society fails and justice isn't served, the adults decide to take matters into their own hands. As Marge points out, the
kids Freddy murdered were from the neighborhood, children they
all knew and loved. When Freddy went free on a technicality, that
didn't sit well with them, so they locked him in his warehouse and
burned it down. After that, they went on with their lives and acted as
if nothing happened. They didn't tell their children, hoping the past
would just disappear. Even when Freddy starts attacking and Nancy
tries to explain it to her mother, instead of trying to help by telling
her about the past, she sends her to an institute, thinking she's a little
crazy. Marge dies because she still doesn't believe Freddy was after
the kids and didn't give her child the information she needed to take
care of the menace.

In *Scream*, the parents are largely absent or having affairs. The
nuclear family has been destroyed because the parents are too concerned with their own desires instead of taking care of their kids.
Billy feels that if he wants to have his family back, he has to make
the offenders pay. He does this by killing Sidney's mother and then
a year later, trying to frame her father for the murder of the teens.
Dewey is supposed to represent both the adult world and social
boundaries through his role as a sheriff's deputy, but he is ineffectual, portraying the adult world as grotesque. No one takes him
seriously, and he can't protect his sister or Sidney. He even gets
stabbed in the back by the killer. The same can be said for Gale. She
comes to the town looking for a good story, not really caring if she
upsets anyone, especially Sidney. This is evident when she plants

Gale (Courteney Cox) and Dewey (David Arquette), two ineffectual adults from *Scream*. *Dimension/Photofest © Dimension Films*

the camera in the house. They know the killer is in there, they know he is after the kids, but they can't do anything about it because the camera has a delay and it's too late. Gale is able to redeem herself by shooting Billy, but she doesn't actually kill him, again reinforcing her ineffectiveness.

The adult world in these films is set up as incredibly grotesque and hung up on the past. They are unable to move forward and get on with their lives, but it is the killer who fails to recognize the fact that the teens he is killing had nothing to do with what happened in the past. There is a mentality here that all teens are just the same and are only concerned with instant gratification; for the most part, this is true, and it doesn't always have to be the killer who believes this. In *Halloween*, when Laurie and Annie stop to talk to Mr. Brackett about a break-in at a store, he claims that it was probably kids. Annie responds by calling him a cynical father who blames everything on kids. In *Friday the 13th*, when the police officer makes his way to Camp Crystal Lake to see if Ralph was there, he asks Jack what he's been smoking, implying that he might have been smoking marijuana. When Jack answers that he doesn't smoke because it causes cancer, the cop launches into a list of the different names marijuana can be called. When Ned asks his other friends what the cop is talking about, sounding as if he really has no idea, the officer tells him to not get smart. Despite the fact that Ned is dancing around in his underwear and feathers and the other teens aren't working, they are not doing anything wrong, but the officer assumes they are just because they are teens.

The killers exert their power over the teens in the harshest way possible, forcing the teens to react to their actions, many times using the same type of violence against the adults as they used on them. When this happens, the teens, or more often the Final Girl, become "reaggregated" into society. By doing this, she takes the most powerful and dominant discourse in the film, makes it her own, defeats the grossly exaggerated teacher, and gains the power in the process.

Within the realm of the film, this usually happens when the sun rises or the police and paramedics come to take the Final Character back to civilization. In *Psycho*, this occurs when Norman is captured and everyone is sitting in the police station listening to the psychiatrist explain Norman's actions. In *Black Christmas*, this happens when the cops find Jess in the basement. In *Texas*, Sally climbs into the back of a truck that speeds down the road. In *Halloween*, Dr. Loomis shoots Michael. Alice decapitates Mrs. Voorhees at the end of *Friday the 13th*, then gets into a canoe and heads onto the lake. When she wakes up the next morning, sheriff's officers are waiting for her on the bank. Freddy disappears in *Nightmare* when Nancy turns her back on him, and Sidney puts a bullet in Billy in *Scream*.

But even with all of these endings, there is an uneasiness because the killer is never really vanquished. Norman's mother's personality completely takes over Norman's mind, and there is an indication he might be found innocent because of insanity. The killer in *Black Christmas* is never found. Sally may have gotten away from the deranged family, but she leaves Leatherface on the side of the road, angrily revving his chain saw. When Dr. Loomis looks out the window to see Michael's body, it isn't there. Alice may have killed Mrs. Voorhees, but Jason is still out there, threatening to pick up where his mother left off. Freddy still exists in the dream world, and a new killer dons the costume and continues to go after Sidney in the second *Scream*. The films leave themselves open so that the rite-of-passage process can occur over and over again, just like it does in real life, and there are always teenagers who need to learn what actions are necessary to function in the adult world. Yet, in slasher films, the Final Character rarely makes it back to society, which means that there is something wrong with the ritual process.

Conclusion

For a teen to pass from childhood into adulthood, they have to be taught the skills and traits they will need to be productive members of society. Slasher films show the process of this passage and the phases the teens must go through, including separating from society, negotiating gender, and turning normal expectations upside down. In the context of the films, the teens don't want to be a part of the society the killers represent, so they try to fight against it and enact social changes. Unfortunately, these lessons and skills do not translate over into society as a whole. First of all, most of the teens are dead, so they would not be able to influence changes in society at all, and, second, we never really see the Final Girl return to society unless it is in the context of needing medical attention. Whatever actions they were involved in during the rites of passage stays there. As a comment on the society that is watching the film, the story that is portrayed is not a conservative one, but one that tries to change how culture is perceived. The film portrays an image of what culture could be like, which is why a female is cast as the hero, but there is also that separation between the audience and the action taking place that allows them to distance themselves from what is happening onscreen.

Notes

1. "The first phase of separation clearly demarcates sacred space and time from profane or secular space and time (it is more than just a matter of entering a temple—there must be in addition a rite which changes the quality of time also, or constructs a cultural realm which is defined as 'out of time,' i.e., beyond or outside the time which measures secular processes and routines). It includes symbolic behavior—especially symbols of reversal or inversion of things, relationships and processes secular—which represents the detachment of the ritual subjects (novices, candidates, neophytes or 'initiands') from their previous social statuses." Victor Turner, *From Ritual to Theatre: The Human Seriousness of Play* (New York: Performing Arts Journal Publications, 1982), 24.

2. "During the intervening phase of transition, . . . the ritual subjects pass through a period and area of ambiguity, a sort of social limbo which has few (though sometimes these are most crucial) of the attributes of ei-

ther the preceding or subsequent profane social statuses or cultural states." Turner, *From Ritual to Theatre*, 24.

3. "Among themselves, neophytes tend to develop an intense comradeship and egalitarianism. Secular distinctions of rank and status disappear or are homogenized." Victor Turner, *The Ritual Process: Structure and Anti-Structure* (New York: Aldine De Gruyter, 1995), 95.

4. Vera Dika, *Games of Terror:* Halloween, Friday the 13th, *and the Films of the Stalker Cycle* (London: Associated University Presses, 1990), 71.

5. Carol J. Clover, *Men, Women, and Chain Saws: Gender in the Modern Horror Film* (Princeton, N.J.: Princeton University Press, 1992), 48.

6. "With changing sexual mores, neither the audience of the late seventies nor the members of the film's community consider the girls' action to be debased or 'dirty.' Instead their actions present them as markers for a 'new sexuality' or, more appropriately, as impoverished or degraded examples of the 'new woman.'. . . In fact, it is primarily their mannish or aggressive attitude that is deemed unacceptable in the film. . . . They want sex now/all the time, and there is little emotional need or 'love' associated with their desires. . . . The film presents Annie and Lynda as grotesque parodies of the type of female they intend to represent. . . . They are parodies of 'new women,' sexually aggressive but ridiculous and, so, easily expendable." Dika, *Games of Terror*, 45–46.

7. "But the fact remains that in most slasher films after 1978 (following *Halloween*), men and boys who go after 'wrong' sex also die. This is not the only way males die; they also die incidentally, as girls do, when they get in the killer's way or try to stop him, or when they stray into proscribed territory. . . . Boys die, in short, not because they are boys, but because they make mistakes." Clover, *Men, Women, and Chain Saws*, 34.

8. Dika, *Games of Terror*, 71.

9. "The fact that horror film so stubbornly figures the killer as male and the principal as female would seem to suggest that representation itself is at issue—that the sensation of bodily fright derives not exclusively from repressed content, as Freud insisted, but also from the bodily manifestations of that content.

"Nor is the gender of the principals as straightforward as it first seems. The killer's phallic purpose, as he thrusts his drill or knife into the trembling bodies of young women, is unmistakable. At the same time, however, his masculinity is severely qualified: he ranges from the virginal or sexually inert to the transvestite or transsexual, and is spiritually divided ('the mother half of his mind') or even equipped with vulva and vagina. . . . In this respect, slasher killers have much in common with the monsters of classic horror-monsters who, in Linda Williams's formulation, represent not just 'an eruption of the normally repressed animal sexual energy of the civilized male' but also the 'power and potency of a non-phallic sexuality.' To the extent that the monster is constructed feminine, the horror film thus expresses female desire only to show how monstrous it is." Clover, *Men, Women, and Chain Saws*, 47.

10. "While Michael does not exhibit any explicit supernatural powers, he does seem to exert an unnatural influence over the events. When Annie is sorting out her dirty shirt in the laundry room, the door slams mysteriously shut and locks itself. After Laurie escapes from Michael and locks herself into the Doyle residence, the side door is suddenly revealed to be open. The most dramatic display of these unstated powers occurs in the 'room of horrors' sequence. After Laurie enters the Wallace residence in search of her friends, she finds Annie dead on the bed beneath the head-stone of Michael's slain sister. As she recoils in horror, the closet door springs open revealing Linda's [*sic*] dead body. Then, as Laurie pulls away, the body of Linda's boyfriend swings out from another closet. Barring the construction of an elaborate mechanism of springs and pulleys in the few minutes between Linda's death and Laurie's entrance, the sudden opening of doors and dropping of bodies occurs through some supernatural means." Kendall R. Phillips, "*The Exorcist* (1973) and *The Texas Chainsaw Massacre* (1974)," in *Project Fears: Horror Films in American Culture* (Westport, Conn.: Praeger, 2005), 136.

LESSON FOUR
NEVER FEEL SYMPATHY
FOR THE KILLER

O ne purpose of the slasher killer is to pass knowledge from
one generation to the next. His is symbolic of society's desire to pass on morals and virtues. But this process doesn't
occur like it's supposed to. The teens aren't interested in what the
teachers are teaching. Plus, the killers' morals and values come from
a past that never existed. In the original films, the audience was
never given too much insight into the killers' motives. Yes, they
were traumatized by an event, but, in some cases, that event isn't
always clear (e.g., *Black Christmas*, *Halloween*). The remakes try to
emphasize the traumatic event, give more details, and maybe make
the audience feel a little sorry for the killer. The remakes humanize
the killer so the audience can relate to him.

Creating Sympathetic Killers

The best example of this can be seen in *Halloween*. In the 1978 version, Michael kills his sister and her boyfriend after having sex, but
we never find out why. In the 2007 version, the first half of the film
is dedicated to explaining why. It takes the audience into Michael's
childhood and shows us his unhappy family life. In the 1978 version,
there are indications that the act of sex is what throws Michael into

111

his murderous rampage, and that carries over into the 2007 version as well.

Society's ideal was that teens were not having intercourse before marriage and that all parents were married. The 2007 version shows us this is not the case. Michael's biological father is gone and has been replaced by an abusive, nonworking stepdad. His mother has to support the family, and to do this she works as a stripper. His sister, even though their mother tells her to take him trick-or-treating, blows Michael off so she can have sex with her boyfriend. At one point, the stepfather even comments on how sexy his stepdaughter is to her mother. Everything this family does is outside of accepted social boundaries, and Michael's murdering spree is the result of that. As Dr. Loomis explains, he is the product of both biological and environmental factors.

The film tries to elicit sympathy from the audience because Michael had no control over where he was born or the makeup of his genes. As a ten-year-old, the only thing he desired was a loving and caring family, but he didn't get that. His reactions to their actions could be justified; a person can only take so much abuse before they snap. As time goes on, even though Michael has been in the mental institution for over fifteen years and will never get better, he has become docile in his surroundings. He sits in his room and creates masks. He isn't hurting anybody. Then, the custodian and his cousin come crashing into his world with their criminal activities. Michael's reaction to their debauchery is justified.

By delving into Michael's past, the audience is given insight into the things that shaped him into a killer. We feel sympathy for him because of the abuse he endured and his inability to change the situation. However, as the film progresses, we learn that sympathy is wasted on Michael. Despite his rough childhood, he is given opportunities to change, but he doesn't. He even kills people who were nice to him. It becomes apparent that Michael murders because he enjoys it.

The other film that takes us deeper in the killer's mind is *Black Christmas*. In the 1974 version, the audience never really knows why

Billy kills the sisters. In the 2006 version, we get a full explanation. Like the remake of *Halloween*, the remake of *Black Christmas* spends half the film in the killer's past. We learn the reason Billy kills is because he was hated by his mother and locked in the attic. His father showed him affection, but his mother takes that away from him by killing the dad. Again, the ideals of mother and father become convoluted. After his father's death, a new man moves in, but it's unclear if his mother and this man ever get married. At one point, he is even sexually abused by his mother and fathers a child. When his mother devotes more attention to his sister than him, he becomes jealous. He wants to be a part of the family, so he sneaks downstairs and kills his mother and stepfather.

Billy was born with a liver disease, which caused his skin to be yellow. His mother never considered him to be the ideal child. She also hates her husband, so instead of leaving the family, she emotionally abandons them and physically locks Billy in the attic. The audience can't help but feel sorry for Billy. His mother verbally chastises him and doesn't buy him gifts on Christmas. The only person who cares about him is his father, and he has to sneak around behind his wife's back to show his son any love. To make Billy's life even worse, Billy's mother and her lover take away the only person who cared for the yellow child.

As time progresses and Billy's life doesn't get any easier, the audience becomes even more repulsed, and feelings of sympathy grow deeper for Billy when his mother sexually abuses him and they create a child together. Billy's mother then focuses all of her love and caring on Agnes. Billy's jealousy and loathing reaches its boiling point, and he comes down from the attic to kill his family. By this point, the audience is on Billy's side and thinks his actions are justified. His mother deserves what she gets.

Even poor Agnes deserves sympathy. She never asked to be brought into the world as a product of incest, and even though her mother showered her with love, she was always curious about the boy in the attic. After Billy attacks and maims her, she is sent to an orphanage. No one wants her because she is deformed, so she goes back to the only place she ever experienced love. How can you not feel sorry for her?

As the film progresses and the killers murder the sorority girls, the audience wonders how they could have felt sorry for the two. While they deserved a little compassion for their home life, they don't show it to anyone else. They were given the chance to change, and they refused it. Like Michael, they seem to take pleasure in killing.

Even the remake of *The Texas Chainsaw Massacre* attempts to give us a little more detail about Leatherface's past. He is no longer referred to as Leatherface, but actually given a name. His family is more intact in the 2003 version with a mother present. After Erin has been captured by the family, his mother explains that she isn't going to let the teens hurt her son anymore. Apparently, Thomas contracted a strange disease that affected his skin and deformed him, which is why he wears masks. The assumption can be made that other teens used to make fun of him, and they paid for it. The implication is that these new teens have also come to make fun of Thomas, so they have to be killed.

How can you not feel sorry for someone who was afflicted with a horrific disease? They didn't ask to be put in that situation, and they can't control how they look. Thomas probably only wanted to be treated the same as the other kids, but when that didn't happen, he took revenge. The family supported him because family always sticks together. Their actions can be justified, to an extent. As the film progresses and the family takes its revenge on people who never even knew Thomas existed, it's hard to continue to feel sorry for them.

In the *Friday the 13th* remake, Jason and his mother just want to be a family again. She kills the counselors to get revenge for his drowning, and he kills teens to get revenge for his mother's death. They were the only family each other had, so they will do anything to get back together. Jason refuses to kill Whitney because she reminds him of his mother. He desperately clings to the idea that he can have a family again, even if he has to keep the mother figure chained to a bed.

It's hard not to feel sorry for the two. After all, losing an only child has to be the most devastating thing a mother can experience, and losing a mother has to be the most awful thing a child can experience. The teens took everything away, and the pair deserves their vengeance. However, they are taking their notions of revenge out on teens who had nothing to do with the original deaths. Again, like the other killers, they are offered the chance to change and to show mercy, but they refuse. The audience's sympathy quickly dissipates when they realize the killers murder for enjoyment.

The remake of *A Nightmare on Elm Street* also tries to show that the killer is misunderstood. As more and more teens die, it is Nancy and Quentin's desire to find out about the past. Their research brings them back to the day care they attended as children and brings knowledge of Freddy. The parents believed that Freddy was sexually abusing the children, but they never received concrete proof. With little evidence to take to the authorities and the desire to not put their children on the witness stand, they took matters into their own hands. Upon hearing the story, Quentin and Nancy are not convinced Freddy did anything wrong. In one conversation with his dad, Quentin makes the comment that they were six at the time—they would have told their parents anything. It then becomes Nancy and Quentin's mission to make things right with Freddy, and the audience wants them to succeed. They want to know that Freddy isn't that bad.

As Nancy and Quentin dive into the past, the audience is also able to see how much pleasure Freddy derived from the kids at day care. He plays with them and takes an interest in their artwork. When the parents go after him, we see how afraid he is. He is cornered in a boiler room, wondering exactly what he did wrong. The parents viciously and cruelly set the place on fire, and Freddy dies horribly, maybe even innocently. The audience sympathizes for his need for revenge and roots him on in his search for justice. Yet that

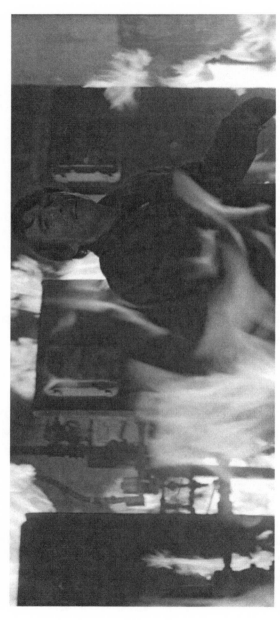

Fred Krueger (Jackie Earle Haley) trapped and frightened in the boiler room in *A Nightmare on Elm Street* (2010). *New Line Cinema/Photofest © New Line Cinema*

sympathy quickly disappears when we discover Freddy was actually sexually abusing the children and takes sadistic pleasure in murdering them.

The remake of *Psycho* is the same as the original, so Norman doesn't get a new or in-depth past, but the audience still feels sorry for him. He was a sad little boy who lost his father when he was very young, and had only his mother for several years. When she found a new lover, he felt abandoned. The audience feels sorry for him because he only wanted to be with his mother, but she left him for her own selfish needs. It was justifiable for him to kill her and her lover to make them pay for how they made him feel. Since the guilt was so much and his desire to have his mother around was so strong, it's understandable he would incorporate her personality into his. The audience loses sympathy for Norman when he attacks and kills Marion. Again, he is given the opportunity to show mercy and compassion, but he doesn't. The jealous, motherly side of his personality has become too dominant. While it is sad Norman is insane, he brought it on himself, so it is hard to feel sorry for him.

Whether the films delve more deeply into the past or reiterate the one that has already been created, the goal is the same: to show how destructive society has become. It also tries to make the audience feel sympathy for the killer. After all, he's only trying to right the wrongs that were done to him. The idea of making the audience sympathize with the killer is not new. In the originals, the director tried to accomplish this by forcing the audience to see things through his perspective; hence the first-person camera work. But to make the films appealing to a new audience, they had to change things up, thus giving the killer an in-depth history. This approach gives the illusion that society has destroyed the killers the same way it has destroyed the teens. The audience may start to believe that the killer is just misunderstood. This is especially evident in *Halloween*. Michael came from a dysfunctional, abusive family. His reaction was to kill those who were oppressing him. His mother and baby sister survived because they didn't do anything wrong to him; they were always loving and supportive. The audience can understand and sympathize with Michael's need to kill those who hurt him.

Billy in *Black Christmas* kills his mother and stepfather after all the abuses they put him through. He only wanted to be loved and accepted, but that was taken away from him. He watched as his sister was given everything she ever desired, so he made the adults pay. The audience understands his desire for revenge.

Thomas in *The Texas Chainsaw Massacre* was made into a social outcast because of a disease that he had no control over. Both Jason and Norman were denied their mothers. Freddy may have been falsely accused of a crime he didn't commit. It seems as if society has turned their backs on these killers and forced them into positions where the only way they can survive is through murder. It appears they are just as much victims as the teens they slaughter. But this is not true. They want to return to the past, when their families were whole, despite the fact that it wasn't the ideal situation, and they want those around them, mainly the teens, to be a part of that past. This is why Michael wants to go home and doesn't remember killing his family, and why he tries to kill Laurie when she refuses to be a part of his family. This is why Billy returns to the sorority house and murders the sisters, propping them up around a Christmas tree. This is why Freddy lures the kids back to the day care and they learn he was actually sexually abusing them. This is why Jason keeps Whitney, and this is why Norman keeps his room the same way he did as a little boy. There is nothing sympathetic about the killers. The killers are the representatives of society, and even though they may not have lived in the ideal, conservative past society wanted them to live in, their jobs are still to punish those who don't obey society's rules.

Another reason to not feel sorry for the killers is because they can never die. They may be defeated at the end of the movie, but they are never down for good. In *Psycho*, Norman is left alive, albeit in police custody, and is seen sitting in his room, the mother side speaking in his mind. He's not dead, so if he ever gets out, it's possible he could kill again. At the end of *Halloween*, Laurie shoots

Michael, blood splattering her face. She breaks down into tears, and the world once again seems safe. However, there is a sequel where Michael comes back to get revenge, so she apparently didn't kill him. In *Friday the 13th*, Whitney and Clay push Jason's body into the lake, then sit down on the dock, looking tired. A few minutes later, his body flies out of the water and grabs Whitney. Again, he wasn't killed. In *Nightmare*, Quentin and Nancy have pulled Freddy into the real world and cut off his hand and sliced his throat. After returning from the hospital, Gwen tells her daughter to get some sleep. The image of Freddy appears in a mirror and kills Nancy's mother, while Nancy stands there and screams.

Bogeymen Are Forever

Like the original films, the killers in the remakes function as bogeymen, enforcing society's rules when the teens overstep their bounds. The parents or other authority figures cannot punish the teens, so these killers do it for them. Like the original, Marion in *Psycho* is being punished for acting outside of accepted sexual boundaries. For a more in-depth discussion on this, refer to lesson 2.

By the time the remake of *Black Christmas* was released, the notions of women's roles in society were redefined. The original focused on the sisters as being independent thinkers and not wanting to be defined by a husband. In 2006, it was acceptable for women to think for themselves and be defined by things other than a husband. However, the idea of not returning to the family is still a major issue in the 2006 version, and the girls are killed for acting outside of accepted social roles. For example, none of the sisters at the house want to be with their families for Christmas. Clair is in the process of heading home, sitting in her room wrapping presents, with the notion that she is going to reconnect with her sister, but there is the implication she might not be looking forward to it. She is struggling to figure out what to write on her sister's card, gulping down wine in the process. Dana is sitting on the couch painting her nails and makes a comment about how she'd like to bury a hatchet in her sister's head. Lauren drinks too much and complains about Christmas, talking about its commercialization and basically showing a complete disdain for the holiday. Heather refuses to take part in the traditions, especially the act of buying Billy a present, which the sorority has done for years, claiming traditions are stupid. Megan is upset and refuses to come downstairs because a video of her and her ex-boyfriend having sex has been released on the Internet. These girls are killed because they don't fit into the social notion that Christmas is a time to be with family or follow the holiday's traditions. They would rather spend their time alone or pretend the holiday didn't exist, and they are punished for it. In death, their bodies are forced to participate, which is why the killers pose them around the Christmas tree.

The teens in *Texas* are traveling across Texas without a care in the world. The focus in the first film was on the notion that the teens didn't have jobs and stumbled across a family who lost their only source of income, but that doesn't seem to be the case in the remake. The focus in this film is on the unacceptable behaviors of premarital sex and drugs. Pepper and Andy spend their time in the van kissing, almost to the point of intercourse; the only thing that stops them is that there are other people in the vehicle with them. It becomes evident that they have only known each other for a few days, as Pepper was a hitchhiker they picked up. Pepper and Andy are willing to skip the formalities of actually getting to know one another (and eventually getting married) before giving into their desires. Even Erin and Kemper are outside of accepted social boundaries since they are not married but still living together. Erin hints that she would like to get married, but it's been three years and Kemper still hasn't asked. Yet she still stays with him.

The teens also smoke marijuana, with the exception of Erin. They roll and light up a joint while traveling down the road. They are also returning from Mexico where they have picked up a large quantity of pot to sell. They are killed because their actions are outside of normal social behaviors, but there aren't any parents around to punish them, so the killers take their place.

Michael becomes the discipliner in *Halloween* because no one else will do it. His mother attempted to be the authority figure, but she failed. She would yell at the stepfather for making lewd comments about her daughter and tell him to shut up when he was being mean to Michael, but she never left him. She would clean up his messes when he told her to or allow him to get drunk in the chair while she went to work. When she was called to the school and shown the pictures of the dogs and cats Michael killed, she refused to believe he was capable of doing such heinous acts. She was even aware of what her daughter and her daughter's boyfriend were doing while she was gone, but she never did anything to stop it. Hence, Michael steps in and becomes the punisher for the wrongs enacted by his sister and stepfather.

Sex in this film plays a major role in why Michael kills. He murders the bully after he shows Michael an advertisement of his mother, which is for the strip club she works for, and makes comments about the sexual things he wants to do to her. He kills his sister and her boyfriend because they were too concerned about having sex rather than taking him trick-or-treating. He kills the janitor and his cousin when they come to the asylum to have sex with a new female patient and rape her on Michael's bed. At first, it doesn't seem like he really cares or that he's going to do anything, but when they start touching his stuff and involving him, he kills them. The truck driver is killed after looking at a porn magazine. Lynda and Bob are killed after engaging in intercourse in Michael's house, and Paul is killed while attempting to have sex with Annie.

In essence, these people are all killed after engaging in a socially unacceptable act that no one else will punish them for. But unlike other bogeys, Michael doesn't only punish those who act outside of social boundaries, he also seems to kill indiscriminately. How else would you explain the murders of the janitor that was nice to him or the various nurses and guards at the asylum? It's possible that some of those deaths were collateral damage, something that had to be done for his escape, and the deaths aren't lingered on, they are shown in the aftermath, with the exception of the murder of the janitor. Michael murdered his stepfather because he didn't act like a father was supposed to. He was abusive and unable to work; he wasn't the ideal male role model. The janitor was nice to Michael the entire fifteen years he was in the asylum, but when he is showing the new janitor around, he mentions that he is going to retire in three months. It's possible that Michael murdered him because he was going to leave. The janitor took care of him and tried to make him feel safe, like a father would, but then he was going to abandon him. Since this is not an acceptable way for a father figure to act, he is killed.

Jason in the remake of *Friday the 13th* functions very well as a bogey, and he punishes teens for their sexual indiscretions and their drug use. This is especially evident after the opening sequence. The teens head into the woods for what they believe is a camping trip; however, Wade and Richie are actually looking for a marijuana field. As night falls, Whitney and Mike decide to go for a walk while the others stay at camp. Richie and Amanda decide they are going to engage in sex, so they send Wade away, where he discovers the marijuana crop. While enjoying the aroma of the plant, he runs into Jason and is killed. Jason then goes after Richie and Amanda, and both of them are killed.

Six weeks after this episode, a new group of teens comes up to the lake to partake in partying and premarital sex, and they are killed for breaking social rules. Chelsea and Nolan are killed on the lake. Even though Trent specifically told them not to take the boat out, they don't listen. They are killed for not following the rules. Both Lawrence and Chewie smoke pot and drink excessively, which leads to Chewie falling over and breaking a chair. When Trent tells him to get some tools to fix it, Chewie heads down to the toolshed, where he proceeds to drink more liquor that doesn't belong to him and breaks more stuff. He is punished for not respecting other people's belongings. Lawrence is killed while heading out to find Chewie.

His crimes were smoking marijuana and drinking. Trent and Bree are killed for participating in sex. Their actions are especially bad because Trent is supposed to be Jenna's boyfriend, so he was cheating on her. It's hard to say exactly why Jenna is killed. She seems to be the good girl, doesn't engage in sex, doesn't drink, and is actually trying to help Clay. But she did come up to the lake house with the others, so maybe she was going to engage in socially unacceptable behaviors.

Again, Freddy is a good bogey because he attacks in dreams. In the original film, Freddy killed the teens for the same reason the other killers murdered them: for acting outside of accepted social or sexual behaviors. In the original, Freddy's actions were supposed to keep the teens within the boundaries of innocence and away from sexual desires. But in the remake, the focus is not on sex, the teens don't engage in sexual activity onscreen. It would be difficult to keep them within the bounds of innocence, also, since Freddy sexually abused them as children. The desire, though, is still to return to a time when the children were young, when they did exactly what the adult world told them without question, even if was detrimental to their well-being. This is especially evident when Freddy first attacks. Nancy and Quentin ask their parents what is going on, and the parents explain that Freddy may have been abusing them. They didn't have enough evidence at the time to go to the authorities, so they took matters into their own hands. Nancy and Quentin don't believe their parents. As expected, the teen generation refuses to listen to the authority figures, even though the parents know what they are talking about. Freddy was killed because of his sexual transgressions. Like the original, Freddy killing the teens also punishes the parents. After all, they were the ones who killed him. They have also failed in their task in teaching the teens the skills they need to function as adults. The teens are punished for not listening to the adults when they finally decide to tell the truth.

In slasher films, society's authority is represented in the figure of a cop. Police officers appear in many of the original films and a few of the remakes. Their presence is to show just how ineffectual society is at keeping the teens under control, which is why it is important for the killer to punish the teens. This is evident in the remake of *Halloween*. Sheriff Brackett refuses to believe Michael has come back to Haddonfield, claiming that the dead coyote and the missing headstone are just a prank played by kids. It isn't until he tries to call Laurie's parents and finds his daughter bleeding on the floor that he realizes he has a problem. But he doesn't do anything to stop Michael. He just fades from the film.

Other officers in the film are just as ineffectual. After Laurie finds her friends dead and Annie barely hanging on to life, she calls for help. She is chased by Michael and heads back to Tommy's house. While there, she and the kids lock themselves in the bathroom. Two cops show up to see if they are all right, and they are killed by Michael.

The cop in *Friday the 13th* isn't much help, either. It is obvious Clay has been back to the county where his sister disappeared several times. The officer pulls him over and comments that he should go back home or look for his sister elsewhere, like the other families. He even suggests she may have run away with her boyfriend. Since he can't find any evidence of her whereabouts or a body, he assumes she is not in his jurisdiction. He has to operate within the world of evidence, and when he doesn't have any, he can't do his job. The teens then call him when Jason attacks them at the cabin, and he shows up to help, only to be killed with an arrow through the eye.

The Texas Chainsaw Massacre takes the notion of the officer as a representative of society's authority and twists it. In the 2003 version, the teens need to find a cop because of the dead body in the back of their van. They stop at a local store, and the shopkeeper calls the sheriff for them. She tells them that he is going to meet them at an abandoned mill. Without worrying about why they are meeting him in a secluded area and accepting the explanation Luda May gives them that the sheriff is in the county and won't make it to town for hours, they head over. Eventually, they find out that the sheriff is actually a member of the Hewitt family. He uses his position of authority to gain the trust of the teens then uses it against them and leads them to their deaths. In a sense, this represents just how far society will go to punish the teens for their misdeeds, but it also important to note he wasn't actually part of society, he was just pretending to be. The real cops in the film, the ones who make it to the Hewitt residence after the murders, are unable to apprehend Thomas, and one of the deputies winds up getting himself killed, but they are still able to bring the family's crimes to light.

On one hand, society condemns the killers for their behaviors because they are acting outside of accepted social boundaries, but on the other, society encourages the killers' actions because they punish the teens in ways society can't. This is why the killers are never actually vanquished at the end of the film. Despite the killers' ability to function outside of normal social boundaries, they still follow a highly ordered set of behaviors and act within a specific set of rules.

Famous Killers Are Incredibly Dangerous . . . and Predictable

Several of the slasher killers have become iconic figures. Norman, Leatherface, Michael, Jason, and Freddy are world renowned. Their appearances and weapons of choice are highly recognizable. Leatherface has his chain saw, Jason has his hockey mask and machete, Freddy has his striped sweater and finger gloves. This is because of the rules that govern their appearances in films. Even though the remakes might try to reimagine the story that surrounds these killers, it doesn't change their appearance or how they kill.

Like the originals, the killers are affected by some sort of trauma that dictates their actions. For Norman and Billy, this has been brought on by their relationship with their mothers. In the original *Black Christmas*, the audience never really got an in-depth look at what happened to the killer to turn him evil, but the remake delves deeply into Billy's past. When the audience first meets Billy, he is locked up in a mental institution. An orderly is going to each door, giving the patients their food and wishing them Merry Christmas. Unknown to the orderly, the door to the outside world has been propped open, which allows a man dressed as Santa to enter. As Santa approaches the cell that contains Billy, he comments on how he remembers the crimes. The guard, who sits at the end of the hall, rises from his seat and explains how every Christmas Billy attempts to escape, and every year he fails. He is caught in a reoccurring cycle that dictates that he has to return home for Christmas. Luckily for him, this last time he is successful, and he heads home to continue killing.

Billy isn't the only one that has been affected by the trauma; his sister Agnes has been turned into a killer also. Even though she was the favored one in the family, when Billy came down and dispatched the stepfather and mother, he did try to kill her, but he only ended up maiming her. She was sent to a foster home, and since no one wanted her, she returned to her childhood house. Agnes, like Billy, functions in a specific set of rules.

Both killers witnessed murders and were abused, so it is the only type of life they know. When they return to the house years after being gone, they pick up where they left off—by murdering the sorority sisters. They have a certain power, almost an invincibility, while inside the house. After all, they know the secrets of the abode and how to get from one place to another without being detected. They also seem to be able to survive the fire, even though it consumes the entire dwelling. However, once they leave the safety of the home, they become vulnerable because they are outside of their boundaries and can be killed, which is why Kelli is able to defeat them.

Thomas in *Texas* contracted a skin disease that deformed him. It is implied that others in the community weren't very nice to him and teased him because of his disfigurement, so he found ways to get even, which generally involved killing them. While it seems like the rest of the community has vanished, the Hewitt family is still going strong, and they view any outsider traveling through as a threat, as someone who is coming to make fun of "their boy." To ensure this doesn't happen, they kill anyone passing through.

The exact methods of how they lure their victims is unknown, but it can be assumed the entire family plays a role. Luda May runs the local store, so if anyone needs gas or food, they stop there, and she could lure them in. Sheriff Hoyt pretends to be the law, so if anyone needs help, they would call him and he could lure them in. However the family does it, one thing is for sure: the victims have to come to them, they don't go out of their way to hunt them down. But once the victims are in their town, there's no way to escape.

Aside from thinking every person is there to ridicule Thomas, there really is no explanation of why the family kills. It's possible the family uses them as food, which is implied by the basement where Leatherface does his work, which is described as looking exactly like a slaughterhouse. It would also make sense since the animals they have butchered aren't very fresh and probably not fit for consumption. For example, when Erin and her friends go to Luda May's store to use the phone, the place is stocked with pig heads and various body parts, but how long they've been there is a mystery. By the amount of flies and the teens' reaction to the smell, it's possible they've been there for way too long. It is also implied that Thomas uses the victims to create new masks since his own face has been destroyed by disease.

The film implies that the Hewitt family has taken a lot of victims, but, again, those victims have to come to them, they don't go out of their way to hunt them down. This is evident with the girl walking down the highway. She had been a prisoner of the Hewitt family but somehow managed to escape. Even though she wasn't very far from their residence, they weren't looking for her. It is possible they didn't know she was gone, but that is speculation. Even when the teens try to report the suicide, they have to go find the sheriff at an abandoned mill, he won't come to them. If they wanted, they could have dumped the body on the side of the road and continued on and probably gotten away without the family following.

This is reemphasized at the end of the film when Erin escapes with the baby. Even though she has run over Sheriff Hoyt, the others are left standing at the store with a semi running right next to them, and they don't attempt to go after her. The killers have to function within their specific set of rules, and that means waiting for their quarry to come to them.

Michael is also trapped in a specific set of rules. In the remake, he really doesn't act against anyone until they have done something bad to him. It is implied he has murderous tendencies, but initially, he only acts out those fantasies on animals. As the people around him get more abusive, he can no longer contain his rage. After he has been committed to the mental institution, it is apparent that Michael is becoming more and more withdrawn from society, hiding behind masks and living inside his own mind. He isn't a threat to anyone. He becomes agitated and murderous when he perceives someone as a threat, which is what happens when the nurse makes a snide comment about the picture with him and his baby sister. The nurse comments that the baby is really cute and there's no way she can be related to him. Michael takes that as an insult to his family, so he stabs her with a fork.

As he grows older, he is content to sit in his room and create his masks. When the janitors come in to take him to his appointment, the older one explains to the new one that Michael doesn't like his stuff to be touched, and as long as he follows those rules, Michael won't harm them, and that's true. However, the young janitor isn't one for following rules, which is evident when he sneaks his cousin into the hospital to rape a female patient. For whatever reason, they think it will add to the excitement if they do it in Michael's room. At first, Michael could not care less. He is lost in his own world creating his masks. But the two men start to mess with his stuff; they break the rules, so he kills them and uses the opportunity to escape.

When he makes it back to Haddonfield, he kills the teens only after they have broken a rule. Lynda and Bob are killed for having sex in his house. Annie and Paul are attacked and Paul is killed for the same reason. Laurie is the only one who survives because she doesn't start out breaking rules. She is the good girl in the film, the one who follows the rules and doesn't participate in premarital sex or underage drinking. But that is not the only reason Michael is interested in her. Michael returns home because he wants to have his family back, and Laurie is his only surviving family. Unfortunately, she doesn't know that. He kidnaps her and takes her back to his old house, showing her the picture of him holding her as a baby. She doesn't know what he is trying to tell her and perceives him as a threat because he has murdered her friends. To escape his grasp, she attacks him with his knife. She breaks the rules and becomes a threat, so Michael goes after her.

In the remake of *Friday the 13th*, Jason wants to be left alone. Or at least that's what the locals tell Clay as he is searching for his sister. Yet, he is out seeking revenge on teens who venture too close to Camp Crystal Lake. It is possible that if the teens would just leave the decrepit, rotting camp alone, Jason might fade back into obscurity. If anyone ventures into his neck of the woods, they will die. The first set of teenagers die because they are camping too close to the camp and engaging in sexual activity, and plan on using the field of marijuana they are looking for to turn a profit. Six weeks after the first deaths, the second set of teenagers are killed because they are still too close to Camp Crystal Lake. Like the family in *Texas*, Jason doesn't leave the territory to find his victims, he waits for them to come to him.

Jason's original drive to kill is to avenge his mother's death. As time goes by, this desire is replaced by a general hatred of the teen generation. Yes, the teens are close to Camp Crystal Lake, but the properties they are at have probably been around the lake and camp for years and never experienced any issues from Jason. Jason no longer kills for revenge or because the teens have ventured too close to his home, he punishes them for acting outside of accepted social boundaries. This is especially true of the farmhand who is killed in the hayloft. When Clay first comes to the property to find his sister, the man is in the barn feeding wood into the chipper. From the looks of the place, it has been around for a long time, and the owner never seemed to have had any problems with Jason. However, because the farmhand is involved in drugs and strange sexual practices involving a mannequin, he is punished.

The parents around Camp Crystal Lake are absent, which means Jason has to take their place. He punishes the teens for their misdeeds, but he can only punish those in his immediate vicinity. However, that means that anyone who ventures into his territory is fair game, including local authority figures.

Freddy in *A Nightmare on Elm Street* can only attack teens in their dreams. Again, like so many other killers, the teens have to venture into his world to be brought to justice. Since everyone has to sleep and everyone dreams, it is impossible not to be a part of Freddy's world. Freddy is not punishing the teens for acting outside of accepted social boundaries, he is using the teens to punish the parents.

In the remake, the teens have no idea who Freddy is or the abusive situation they were put through as children. The parents have gone out of their way to make sure the teens never have to relive the hardships and embarrassment of their childhood years. They've even gone so far as to murder another human being. Instead of punishing the parents directly for their wrongdoings, Freddy decided to go after the children. It is important that he goes after them in their teen years because of the social implications. They are right on the verge of still being children, yet almost adults. While it was important for the parents to teach them the skills they would need to function as adults, they aren't quite ready to be on their own. By taking them away from the parents at this critical juncture, it symbolizes the parents' failure to properly equip their kids with the skills their children need to survive.

Teens are naturally defiant toward parental or authority figures. They think they've figured it all out and don't need any more help. They question what their parents have done. Freddy has done a great job of casting doubt and suspicion on the teens' parents' motives. He has portrayed himself as an innocent who became the victim of circumstance. To find the truth, Nancy and Quentin completely disregard everything their parents told them and take it upon themselves to prove Freddy's innocence. In a way, he draws them into his world. However, as they delve deeper into the past, Nancy and Quentin discover that Freddy isn't as innocent as he portrayed himself and all the things he was accused of doing, he actually did. By this point, though, they have alienated themselves from their parents and their protective custody. They are on their own and must figure out how to defeat Freddy.

Freddy can only attack the teens in their dreams; he is limited by his specific set of rules. Despite these limitations, he is a powerful force that is difficult to defeat. He can bend the rules any way he wants within his own social boundaries, and that is how he is able to defeat the teens. To defeat Freddy, Nancy has to physically pull him out of the dream world and into her world, where his rules no longer apply. But even then, he is never down for good.

The Killers' Past Comes Back to Haunt Them

The actions of the killers in these films are generally governed by an outside force that dictates the standard of behavior, usually a parental or authority figure. Since the killers are supposed to represent the idealized past, they turn to figures from their past that influenced them the most. For example, in the remake of *Black Christmas*, Billy was abused and abandoned by his mother. Then, she killed his father. The only life he's known is one full of hardship and death. When given the opportunity, he uses what he's been taught by his mother to kill. He begins by murdering his family, then moves on to anyone else who gets in his way. At one point in the film, one of the characters makes a comment about how killing might be the only way Billy knows how to show love, which may or may not be true. It is certain that it's the only way he can get people around his Christmas tree.

Billy's mother was cruel and sadistic, so Billy becomes cruel and sadistic. She set the precedent for how he would act, and he follows just like he was taught. These actions also affect his sister, who grew up in the same household. The past repeats itself through the generations because no one has lived any differently. The only thing that can break the cycle is the death of the killer, which is accomplished by the Final Girl.

In *The Texas Chain Saw Massacre*, it is evident that the family has been involved in killing for generations. In the 1974 version, this was because the slaughterhouse was closed and they needed to do something for food. In the 2003 version, this may be the case, but it's never really explained. There are hints that the family kills because people made fun Thomas when he was a child, but it's really left to speculation exactly why they murder. In either case, it's evident that the murders have been occurring for a long time. The Hewitts' property is covered with the relics of the past: old cars and suitcases. Sheriff Hoyt also seems to know exactly what he is doing when he lures the teens to his house. The same can be said for Henrietta and her friend. As soon as Erin bursts through their door, hysterical from being chased by Leatherface, they just calmly hand her a cup of tea that has been laced with a sleeping drug. Each and every member of the family knows what they have to do to ensure that victims don't escape.

Thomas seems to be the best at what he does because he actually performs the murders. While the rest of the family lures the victims to the house, Thomas takes them to the basement and carves them up. Obviously, he learned his skills while working in the slaughterhouse since the basement is set up like the killing floor. He is meticulous in his work, even though he's not excessively concerned with clean or sanitary conditions. It's obvious he's been doing his job for a long time, but it's not obvious who taught him how to do it. It can be assumed it was his mother, since she runs the local store that is filled with rotting animal parts.

Even Jedidiah knows what to do when luring the victims, even if he doesn't participate in the murders yet. When the teens drive to the abandoned mill to wait for the sheriff, they find Jedidiah hiding in the building. Instead of warning them, telling them to get away, he engages them in conversation, making it possible for the sheriff to arrive. Later, when Erin is trapped in the basement of the house, he does help her escape, but she is the only surviving member of her group at this point. Jedidiah seems to be the outsider in the family. After Erin has been captured, he watches from the front window as they tease and taunt her on the living room floor. He asks if he can come in the house, but Luda May tells him he has to stay out with the dogs. Perhaps this is why he helps Erin escape; perhaps he is trying to get even with his family. Even though Jedidiah has moments of being helpful, he is still a member of the family. He's still seen the killing firsthand, and, given enough time, he'll probably become more involved, just like Thomas.

The family has a tradition of working together to subdue their victims. Each member has a role, and those roles have more than likely been passed from generation to generation. They count on outsiders stumbling into their neck of the woods, then they make sure they never leave. It is obvious this cycle would continue to propagate, especially with the presence of children and the fact that Thomas Hewitt is never captured. However, Erin is able to break the cycle by taking back the baby the family kidnapped and informing the real authorities of what the family is doing.

Again, in the *Halloween* remake, the parental generation sets up the basis for Michael's actions. Michael's home life is much less than ideal: he lives with an abusive stepfather, his sister is mean and sexually active, and his mother is a stripper who tries to keep everyone happy and together. It is easy to see how his sister's torments and his stepfather's cruel words have emotionally scarred Michael as a young boy. Unlike in other slasher films, his mother is very loving and caring toward him. Even after he massacres the majority of his family, she still comes to visit him in the mental institution. When the principal calls her into the office and shows her the pictures of the animals he's tortured and killed, she refuses to believe her son is capable of such actions. Even though all the signs are there, Deborah refuses to believe her son is capable of murder. In essence, she turns a blind eye to his actions, making it that much easier for him to commit his crimes.

Deborah's actions, or lack thereof, influence Michael's reactions to certain situations. Where she is passive and allows others to take advantage, Michael becomes aggressive and exerts his authority. For example, when the bully at school taunts and teases him in the school bathroom, making lewd comments about Michael's mother, Michael hunts him down after school and beats him to death with a tree branch. The same type of thing occurs when Michael murders both his sister and stepdad. Deborah is getting ready to go to work, and she tells her husband and daughter the rules for when she's gone, but they ignore her. Since she's not there to enforce the rules, Michael takes it on himself to punish them. These actions carry through to his adult years when he escapes from the asylum.

At the beginning of the remake of *Friday the 13th*, Jason sees his mother beheaded by a camp counselor on the shore of Crystal Lake. Even though he was supposedly already dead, he returns from the grave to avenge his mother's death. Like his mother, he punishes teens for acting outside of accepted social norms. Even though his mother hasn't been around to raise him, she still influences his actions.

Jason desires to have his family back and keeps Whitney because she looks like his mother. She is the only person he won't kill, and he keeps her chained in his home. Until Whitney starts to fight back, Jason is content to let her survive. His mother's distrust and hate for teens, coupled with Jason witnessing his mother's death, is what drives Jason's behavior.

In the *A Nightmare on Elm Street* remake, it is a little more difficult to know what parental/authority influence affected Freddy's behavior. The audience doesn't get to see Freddy's home life and past. The only past they return to is when Freddy abuses the children and is killed by their parents. However, his actions are repeated through time and influence how others around him respond. Freddy sexually abused the teens when they were children, and when he was punished for it, he vowed to come back and make them pay when they were older. Not only is he getting back at the teens, he is also getting back at the parents who killed him. He stalks and kills the teens in their dreams because it is the only place the parents can't protect them. Even though his method of stalking and killing the teens is a little harsher than sexually abusing them, the process is still the same. He tries to gain their trust, luring them into a false sense of security, then he strikes the fatal blow. The only way for the teens to survive his attacks is to break his cycle, which is accomplished by bringing Freddy out of the dream world and into the real world.

The parental/authority figures affect how the killers in the film are supposed to act, but they are also influenced by the genre and the original films. When the movies first came out in the 1970s and 1980s, they created a huge following. Audience members connected with the killers, and the majority of them became world renowned. Because of their popularity, directors and writers knew they couldn't completely change the killers in the remake. Both new and old audience members had expectations of how the killers were supposed to act. This is especially evident in how the killers look and their methods of killing the teens. Leatherface is recognized by his apron, mask, and chain saw. Michael is known for his white mask and coveralls. Audience members recognize Jason because of his hockey mask and machete, and Freddy is known for his striped sweater, hat, and finger knives.

In the majority of these films, the director has taken scenes or lines directly from the original version. This not only pays homage to the original films, but it reinforces how static the genre is and how much the message of these films hasn't changed. For *Psycho*, the new director changed very little. Having the film shot in color was the biggest alteration, as well as adding a few things for clarity and making Marion a stronger Final Girl. Otherwise, the film is a carbon copy of the original. In *Texas*, even though the director tries to give a little more backstory and explain in more detail why the Hewitt family kills, it copies murders directly from the 1974 version. When Andy is killed, he is maimed and loses a leg, but then Leatherface hangs him on a meat hook, which is reminiscent of Pam's death in the original. The fact that Thomas continues to use a chain saw and chases Erin through a slaughterhouse also reflects scenes from the original.

In the original *Black Christmas*, the audience never gets the chance to see the killer, only bits and pieces of him, but that doesn't stop the director in the remake from bringing back elements from the 1974 version. The most recognizable of these is the crystal unicorn that was used to kill Barb in the original. The figurine makes an appearance in the 2006 version and is used to stab and kill other victims, most notably Lauren, who, like her predecessor, is stabbed after passing out from too much alcohol.

In *Halloween*, Michael killing his sister after she has intercourse with her boyfriend is on course with the 1978 version. Michael wears his stereotypical white mask and coveralls, and uses a butcher knife to carry out the majority of the murders. Deaths that are repeated in this film that are reminiscent of the original include Bob's death, where he is pinned to the wall with a butcher knife, and when Michael goes to find Lynda dressed as a ghost wearing Bob's glasses. Just the very fact that Michael returns to Haddonfield and kills teens on Halloween points back to the original film.

In *Friday the 13th*, Jason wears his iconic hockey mask (although in the 2009 version, it takes almost half of the film before he finds and puts it on) and carries his trademark machete. Deaths that are repeated in this film include the machete across the face, arrows piercing people's eyes, and people being impaled to walls with sharp objects.

In *Nightmare*, the audience is able to instantly recognize Freddy because of his finger knives and mutated face. The film reproduces the death scene in which Tina is thrown about the room and murdered while her boyfriend watches. In the 2010 version, Kris is killed in almost exactly the same way while her boyfriend Jesse watches, and then he is killed after falling asleep in prison, just like his counterpart Rod. The bathtub scene with Nancy is even repeated in the 2010 version.

There are elements in each of these films that have been changed, but they are only there to keep the movie fresh and keep the audience interested. Each of these franchises sets certain standards for the genre, and audiences expect to see those when they go to the film. The original films set the standards for what is expected to occur in the films; that is how they gained and maintained their popularity. If the new films deviate too far from the original behaviors, the director risks alienating audience members.

Don't Trust the Killers' Lessons

The killers in these films are supposed to represent the idealized past, even if they made that past up, and they are supposed to be teachers that pass wisdom down from one generation to the next. The remakes of the films show that the killers' parental/authority figure generation has succeeded in passing the wisdom to their children, but the killers cannot pass their wisdom to the teen generation. Like the originals, these films show how ritual has failed. Each of these films functions in a very static state, where the teens and the killers have to function within certain rules. The killers try to return to an ideal, fictionalized past, and the teens fight against that return.

Again, the setting of these remakes plays an important part in the ritual and the teens' liminality. In *Psycho*, the Bates Motel is still off the main highway and has to be traveled to. Since the film didn't deviate from the original, refer to lesson 2 for an in-depth discussion on this topic.

The setting of *Black Christmas* takes place once again in a sorority house, but the place has been given a different history. Before it was converted to be a part of the university, it was a family home.

After the murders, the house sat empty before the university bought the block. The locals talk about how after the murders, the house was considered haunted. No one wanted anything to do with it, so it sat unchanged for years. Even after it became a sorority house, the history of the place still dominates how people react to the dwelling. Every year, it is expected that the sisters would buy Billy a Christmas present. They continue to talk about the murders, and model their lives to make sure they wouldn't happen again. Even though it has been years since Billy killed his family and none of the girls in the house are from the town it occurred in, the actions still influence their daily lives. The house is suspended in time, and things only get worse once the murders happen all over again.

The notion of change begins when Heather refuses to buy the traditional Billy Christmas present. The sorority house followed the tradition for years, but she didn't see the point of continuing. This small defiance of tradition leads to other small changes, which eventually leads to the destruction of the house. Since the house is the actual symbol of static, ritual behavior and society, that is where Billy and his sister return to to continue their murdering spree. In order for the Final Girl to break free from the system, she has to physically destroy the house, which occurs when it burns to the ground. After that, the killers can easily be vanquished.

In the 2003 version of *Texas*, the teens aren't traveling to the family's grandparents' house, they are just making their way across Texas after being in Mexico and happen upon a small town. However, like the 1974 version, the town is a static location where things haven't changed much over time. There are pig heads and other slaughtered animals in the store that look like they've been there for a long time. The mill where the teens are supposed to meet the sheriff is falling apart and hasn't been visited in ages. The Hewitts' property is littered with abandoned cars and belongings that are rusting under the Texas sun. Even the slaughterhouse is frozen in time. Tools and carcasses hang from the walls even though it looks like it hasn't been used for years. The family seems more content to kill people than use the frozen slaughtered cows for food. The family also seems content to pass their murderous ways to the next generation, which is evident in Thomas's behavior and Jedidiah's initial actions. It is also implied that the baby the family kidnaps will be taught how to kill. However, things change when Erin fights back.

Whatever she did to influence Jedidiah, it is enough for him to help her escape the basement before Thomas can kill her. Her running away from the family also leads to Thomas injuring himself with his own chain saw and being mortally wounded in the slaughterhouse. Erin is also able to save the baby from the family's influence, and she kills Sheriff Hoyt while escaping. Like the original, her driving down the road in the sheriff's cruiser is symbolic of her ability to move forward. The family is stuck at the store watching as she escapes. They could have gone after her if they were inclined—there was a running semi parked on the street—but they are fixed in a static location, unable to change.

Like the 1978 version, the 2007 version of *Halloween* takes place in the suburbs. Again, Michael's house has become run down and decrepit, but little else has changed. He is stuck in a mind-set that he wants to return to his family and find his baby sister. However, she has grown up and doesn't remember her older brother. She is able to break free from his static world because she was never a part of it. She sees him as a destructive, murdering force, so she fights against him. Like *Black Christmas*, the house in *Halloween* is the symbolic representation of the static time the killer wants to return to. Laurie is able to break free from that place by physically breaking free of the house. She literally falls through the ceiling, then is tackled off the balcony by Michael. Once she is free, she is able to overcome the killer and shoot him in the face.

In the 2009 version of *Friday the 13th*, the summer camp is present, but it doesn't play as important a role as the 1980 version. The teens do visit the camp, but it is falling apart. Jason tries to keep it homey; his bed is intact, along with some toys and a shrine to his mother, but even he has moved to underground tunnels. It is the area around the camp where the majority of the murders take place. Like the summer camp, though, the community around the camp isn't a place that is visited very often, and it is a very static location; things haven't changed much over the years. There are summer properties and cabins, owned by rich people, that aren't visited often. The locals tend to keep to themselves, and they warn anyone who is willing to listen to do the same. While looking for his sister, Clay approaches a house that is tucked back in some trees. The property is littered with trash and seems to have been abandoned. He knocks repeatedly on the door, but no one answers. He decides to leave a flyer, and while he is crouched down, a dog attacks the door. Startled, Clay stands and is confronted by a woman, who is dressed as if she just stepped out of the 1950s. Clay asks if she's seen his sister, and she nonchalantly answers that she's dead. She then cryptically talks about how he just wants to be left alone, then disappears. The same thing happens when Clay visits another ranch. He doesn't actually speak to the owner but to a hand who is chopping wood. Again, the property is littered with trash and looks abandoned. The farmhand can't give Clay any answers but asks if he wants to buy some marijuana. Clay says no and leaves. Later, when the audience goes back to the farm, they see just how run down the property is. Relics of the past litter the attic, and the owner is still nowhere to be found when Jason attacks and kills the help, even after the help has commented on the number of guns the owner possesses.

Crystal Lake is outside of normal social boundaries, and the teens have to travel there. Jason only commits his murders within a small radius of the camp; he doesn't travel outside to find victims. The location hasn't changed much in the past years, and the locals are smart enough to stay out of the way. When they do try to interfere, such as when the cop goes to the cabin to help the teens, they are murdered. However, things can't remain unchanged forever, and this is evident when Clay comes looking for Whitney. She was in Jason's possession for six weeks, and it is unknown if she ever tried to escape. However, when her brother shows up, she has a newfound

Whitney (Amanda Righetti) and Clay (Jared Padelecki) get ready to take on Jason in *Friday the 13th* (2009). *Warner Bros./Photofest © Warner Bros.*

desire to live and fights against Jason. Whitney knows that to defeat Jason, she has to play by his rules. He believes she is his mother, so she has to pretend and play the role long enough to distract Jason. She is able to defeat him and stabs him with his own machete. At the end of the film, instead of leaving, Clay and Whitney roll Jason's dead body into the lake. He, of course, isn't dead, so they are in the perfect position to become his next victims.

Again, in *Nightmare*, Freddy can only attack in dreams. Each teen is brought to Freddy's world, which is a static representation of the boiler room he was killed in. The scene changes sometimes, like when Nancy is being pursued by Freddy in a house, but the rules are always the same: the teens are powerless against Freddy and he controls when and how he will kill them. Since the teens have to fall asleep, Freddy knows he can bide his time and wait for them. He even comments to Nancy that he wanted her to be the last one to fall asleep because then she'd be so tired she wouldn't be able to wake up. By this time, her friends are already dead. Nancy runs and hides from Freddy. It isn't until she has no place left to run that she turns and fights back. By this point, she has been trapped in a bedroom and dressed in clothes she wore as a child. Freddy throws her across the room, and she is able to grab a pair of scissors. She stabs him with them, but since they are in the dream world, they have no effect. It isn't until Nancy is able to pull Freddy into the real world that she can actually harm him. Once there, with a bit of help from Quentin, she is able to defeat Freddy. The only way the teens can defeat Freddy is to take him out of his world and drag him into the real world.

How to Survive

Even though the teens in these movies are fighting against the killers and their desire to return to a static, idealized, fictitious past, they are trapped in their own repetitive system and have their own rituals they have to follow. Like the originals, they have to fight against the killers to ensure that change occurs. However, they are also not allowed to act until they have found their friends' dead bodies. In the remake of *Psycho*, Lila doesn't fight against Norman until after she finds his mother's corpse. Even though Sam does most of the work, she delivers the kick to his face that knocks him out. Kelli doesn't fight back in *Black Christmas* until after she's been in the hospital and knows that all of her sorority sisters are dead. Erin fights Thomas after she sees her friends die, taking him on a wild goose chase through the slaughterhouse. She still does a lot of hiding at this point, but she does attack Leatherface with a meat cleaver. By the end of the film, she is willing to run over the killers with a car to ensure her escape. In *Halloween*, Laurie fights back against Michael only after he kidnaps her and takes her to the basement of his house. While her first attack is just to get away from him, when she realizes hiding isn't going to deter him and he tackles her off a balcony, she then picks up a gun and shoots him in the face. For Clay and Whitney in *Friday the 13th*, they fight back when they get cornered in the barn. Up to that point, even though they find the bodies of their friends or watch them get killed, they don't take action. When they are the last two standing and have no other choice, then they fight back. The same situation occurs in *Nightmare*. Only when Nancy and Quentin are cornered do they realize they have to take action. Until then, they try to make sure someone is always there to wake them up when things get bad. But they know that they can't stay awake forever, so they make a plan to destroy Freddy.

Even though the Final Characters are stuck in their own form of ritual behaviors, they still make it out of the killers' static world, but they don't destroy the killer or his ideal. Even if they make it back to society, they don't come out of the ordeal unscathed or unaffected by the ordeal. In *Psycho*, the audience knows that Sam and Lila make it back because they are seen in the police station, but they are both suffering from the loss of Marion. In *Black Christmas*, Kelli makes it back to society, as represented by her stay in the hospital, but she still has to fight against the killers and has to live with the physical scars they inflict and the mental ones knowing that her sorority sisters are dead. Laurie in *Halloween* is completely affected by Michael's actions. Even though she makes it back to society, her family and friends have all been killed (the second film actually shows how she is not coping with the changes). She is no longer the happy, carefree teen she used to be. In *Texas*, the audience never sees Erin make it back to society. They assume she does because the real authorities start an investigation, but it's unclear how badly she has been traumatized by the death of her friends.

In *Friday the 13th*, Clay and Whitney don't make it back to society at all. The final scene shows them on the dock, and Jason breaks through the wood to attack them. They have been traumatized by their ordeal because Whitney sits on the dock with her knees pulled to her chest. Even Clay has a look of defeat on his face. This is only compounded when Jason jumps from the water and attacks Whitney. In *Nightmare*, the pair supposedly makes it back to society, and the final scene is Nancy at her house with her mother.

However, Freddy appears once again and pulls Gwen through the mirror.

Conclusion

Society wants to pass its ideals, values, and morals on to the next generation. In the context of the remakes, the killers' families have succeeded in doing that, but when the killers try to pass those ideas to the teen generation, it doesn't work. Like the originals before, this causes the killer in slasher films to react, normally in a violent manner, and the teens have to fight for their survival. Both the teens and the killers have to function within a specific set of rules, and these rules and actions define the slasher genre. The repetition of these themes reinforces the ritual that is repeated through time and drives the desires of both the teens and killers.

TEENS NEVER LEARN

Like the originals, the use of teens in slasher film remakes portrays the significance of the teen years. They are still an in-between group, and they still have the freedom of trying to figure out who they are as people. Society still tries to teach the teens the proper ways to act to be functioning adults, and the films portray the rites of passage the teens have to go through to make it to adulthood. The rite is a process with its own rituals and rules, and if the teens can survive, they will become adults. The fact that the remakes are still teaching teens how to function as adults shows that the teens are not very good at learning from the past. After so many years and several generations, they have not learned how to act or defeat the killer easily.

You're on Your Own

Like the originals, the remakes of these films separate the teens from regular society. The setting has a sense of sacredness and places them "out of time" (for more in-depth definition of this, refer to lesson 3). Since most of *Psycho* is a carbon copy of the original, refer to lesson 3 for a discussion on this film.

In the 2006 version of *Black Christmas*, the sorority house has been moved off campus, but it's still not part of regular society. According to Kyle, in the past, the house used to be another family dwelling. After the murders, it remained empty for several years until the university bought it and converted it. The house is outside of normal social boundaries on two counts: 1) because it was a place where murder occurred, which is an act outside of accepted behaviors, and no one in the community wanted anything to do with it; and 2) after it was converted into a sorority house, social rules no longer applied. The girls were allowed the freedom generally associated with college years, which meant they could drink, cuss, and engage in sexual intercourse all they wanted without repercussions from society.

The out-of-time experience comes into play with the rituals that occur in the house. Each generation that comes through is identical to the one before: girls looking to gain an education and have fun in the process. The notion of Christmas is even an out-of-time holiday. Even though it occurs at a specific time during the year, the holiday asks us to return to the past and celebrate the birth of Christ. It has its own traditions, whether social or within family structures, that have been passed down for generations and reoccur every year. The sorority girls place themselves outside of these traditions by refusing to participate in them. The majority of them aren't excited about heading home to be with family, if they are heading home at all. Lauren doesn't believe in the Christmas season and attacks all the traditions or ideals, including commercial and religions ones, that are applied to the holiday. During the Christmas holiday, they are also expected to buy gifts for one another and for Billy. Heather is the first girl in the house's history to shun the tradition and refuse to buy Billy a gift.

In *Texas*, the teens are traveling across a sparsely inhabited area of Texas. This place is outside of normal social boundaries because society consists of the Hewitt family. They have developed their own "law enforcement" system, which is a member of their own family who dresses up like a sheriff's deputy and leads people to their deaths. The out-of-time experience occurs as they cross the countryside. The audience is given a specific date for when the events occurred, August 13, 1973, and Erin tells us that she has been with her boyfriend for three years, but that all seems to fade away as they travel. There is no indication of time; the audience doesn't know if they are there in the morning or afternoon, until the day turns into night, but even then, the night seems to last forever as Erin fights for her life. When they pick up the girl who escaped the family's clutches, they have no idea how long she has been roaming the highway. Time also fades away when they run into the family. The teens are just another set of victims in a long line of travelers who are murdered by Thomas, and their van placed among the rusting ruins of the other cars proves that. The rotting meat in the case in the store also reinforces this point. There are flies and the characters' reactions to the smell indicate it's been there for a while, but how long exactly is unknown. When they are instructed to head to the abandoned mill, it appears it has been out of operation for a while, but exactly how long is never explained. The Hewitt family has been living in the area and murdering people for an undetermined amount of time; they have passed their skill sets on to the younger generation, and the indication is they aren't going to change any time soon. They are out of time because they don't have any influences from outside sources.

In the 2007 version of *Halloween*, like the 1978 version, the film takes place within the boundaries of suburbia. There is no physical separation from society since the film takes place in individual homes, but like the original, there is a sense of sacredness to the house because of the rituals and schedules unique to each family. The out-of-time notion comes into play with Michael and his crimes. Like the original, in the remake, Michael is still committing the same type of crimes he did when he was a child. He also is returning to be with his family, but his younger sister has no memory of him. Again, like the original, the film takes place on Halloween, a holiday that mixes the notions of past and present, dead and alive.

The 2009 version of *Friday the 13th* takes the characters outside of normal social boundaries, much like the original. In the remake, the camp isn't the focus of the murders, but it still plays a role. The first characters in the film travel through the woods looking for a field of marijuana that just happens to be close to Camp Crystal Lake. Whitney and Mike stumble across the camp while on a walk. The buildings' exteriors are falling apart, but the interiors have been frozen in time. Food rots in dishes on the table, and Jason's room is still decorated as if he'd never left. Even in the tunnels, which Jason has made his home, are articles he has kept from his victims. The items are an array of things from the past and present, blurring the notion of time. Jason still believes he is a little boy and can be tricked into listening to his mother, even though she is dead.

Like the original *Nightmare*, the 2010 version uses dreams as the sacred and timeless setting. They are a place the individual can only go when one is asleep, and society has no control over what happens in the mind's eye. The teens are also out of time because they can't remember their past. To protect them, the parents erased all memories of their childhood. They didn't know they knew each other as kids but thought they met as teenagers. Even though Nancy is a teenager, Freddy wants her to still be the little girl he liked so much. As he torments her in her dreams, he dresses her in a dress that she wore when she was little. The past and present mix in a bloodbath of murder.

The separation from society places the teens in an in-between stage, a place where they are learning how to function as adults. It is in this stage that teens are allowed to explore themselves and others freely, and where the idea of gender and how to function as a male or female in society comes into play.

Don't Be a Stereotype

Lesson 3 explored how the original films were condemned and criticized for reinforcing misogynistic ideals. It looked at the arguments of Clover and Dika and how they viewed gender in slasher films. The originals were made between 1960 and 1984, a time when the women's movement was trying to make major social changes. By the late 1990s and early 2000s, women achieved a lot of social victories and were able to change things for the better. For audiences from the late nineties, it wouldn't have been shocking to see a woman as the Final Character. In fact, by this time and in this genre, it was pretty much expected. However, the notion of gender still plays an important role because it is still an important aspect of teens becoming adults. Even though the remakes aren't as shocking or draw as much condemnation as the originals, gender is still an issue in the films.

The ideas of masculine and feminine stereotypes play a huge role in the portrayal of characters and exactly what those definitions mean to society. Lila in *Psycho* fits into the feminine stereotype because she has long hair and she doesn't engage in premarital sex like her sister. However, like the original, she is still unmarried and works outside the home. The remake also emphasizes her independence more than the original; she is outspoken and refuses to take no for an answer. Even though Sam still saves her at the end of the film, she delivers the final kick that knocks Norman out.

The sorority sisters in *Black Christmas* are set up to be ideal females. They all have long hair, they are concerned with how they look, and they sit on the couch and file their nails. However, unlike stereotypical females, they also drink, cuss, and talk badly about their families. Heather doesn't follow traditions, which a "real" woman would have done, and Megan engages in premarital sex.

Kelli seems to be the ideal female because she follows the rules, is responsible, and doesn't have sex with her boyfriend. She even gets upset and breaks up with Kyle when she finds out he video-taped a previous sexual encounter. Her ideals of wholesomeness complement society's ideal of how a woman should act. However, Kelli is stubborn and refuses to listen to Kyle when he tells her it's dangerous to go into the attic. A "real" woman would have obeyed the male figure.

Leigh (Kristen Cloke) with a few of the sorority sisters (Mary Elizabeth Winstead, Michelle Trachtenberg, and Katie Cassidy) in *Black Christmas* (2006). *Dimension Films/ Photofest © Dimension Films; Photographer: Shane Harvey*

Erin in *Texas* tries to be a stereotypical female by being compassionate and caring. She is concerned about the others and wants to make sure they are safe. After the hitchhiker kills herself in the back of the van, despite the fact that the majority of the others want to leave her body on the side of the road, she refuses to let them. When she and Andy go to the Hewitt house to find Kemper, Old Monty falls out of his wheelchair, and she assists him back into his seat, even though it was just an excuse for him to fondle her. Erin rescues the child at the end of the film so the baby doesn't have to be raised by psychopaths. She has long hair and wears tight clothes that show off just how feminine she is. When given the opportunity to partake in smoking a joint, she throws it out the window. Yet she is unmarried and has lived with her boyfriend for the past three years. She stands her ground when it comes to the dead body and convinces the others, albeit reluctantly, to wait for the sheriff.

Laurie in *Halloween* appears to be the stereotypical female, just like the original. She is a good student, obeys her father, doesn't

A very feminine yet tough Erin (Jessica Biel) from *Texas Chainsaw Massacre* (2003). *New Line Cinema/Photofest © New Line Cinema*

have a boyfriend, and doesn't drink. However, she talks openly about sex and teases her mother about a local hardware store owner, who she claims is a pervert, making inappropriate sexual gestures with a bagel.

In *Friday the 13th*, Whitney is very feminine because of her nurturing side. She feels guilty for going camping because she should be at home taking care of her sick mother. She has a boyfriend, but she doesn't engage in sexual activity onscreen with him. She doesn't know they are in the woods to find a field of marijuana, so it can be assumed she doesn't do drugs. After her brother shows up to find her, she no longer remains complacent. She fights back against Jason and actually stabs him with his own machete.

Nancy in *Nightmare* is an artist and very shy. She spends most of her time listening to her iPod and blocking out the world. She doesn't have a boyfriend and is very timid around boys. But she is also dark and brooding. One of the reasons she doesn't have a lot of friends is because she isn't like her peers. Since she keeps mainly to herself, her other classmates view her as odd.

Like the original films, if a character is too masculine or too feminine or if they combine the two traits in socially unacceptable ways, they become victims. It is the ability of the Final Characters to blend these traits correctly, to become ambiguous, that allows them to survive. In the original *Psycho*, Marion was outside of normal social boundaries because of her sexual trysts with Sam. She was punished for having sex outside of marriage and then for stealing the money. In essence, she was punished for behaving in ways that were more suitable to a male. The same thing occurs in the remake. Marion wants to be married, she argues with Sam about it, but when he says it's not feasible, she is willing to go her separate way and find someone who will marry her. While there are feelings involved, she is able to push them aside to get what she wants, a trait that is generally associated with males. Even her hair in the remake is masculine: very short. Her actions lean more toward the masculine side, which means she isn't combining the traits properly, so she is killed.

In the remake of *Black Christmas*, the sorority girls are murdered because they act outside of accepted female stereotypes. Megan engaged in premarital sex that was videotaped. By 2003, a female engaging in premarital sex would not have been shocking, but for it to be broadcast for the world to see, that would have been frowned upon. Lauren is killed for being outspoken and a drunk. Heather dies for not following the rules of the house and for being uncompassionate. But, again, what about Clair? She isn't onscreen long enough for the audience to have a backstory, and we don't see her doing anything except for wrapping gifts. When her sister Leigh shows up, she explains to the others that she and Clair are actually half sisters. She tells them that they have never been close, mainly because of age and their parents, but they are trying to fix that. It is possible that Clair dies because she has started a relationship with her sister, which goes against the wishes of her parents, but we can't know for sure. Dana dies because she has a negative attitude toward her family. Her only desire is to bury a hatchet in her sister's head.

In *Texas*, both men and women die for acting outside of their stereotyped traits. Pepper dies because she is sexually promiscuous. Even though it can be assumed Erin and her boyfriend engage in sexual activity, the audience never sees it onscreen. Pepper flaunts her sexuality. Morgan dies because of cowardice. When Sheriff Hoyt forces him into the van to reenact the suicide, he becomes incredibly upset and begins to cry, an unacceptable trait in a male. When faced with the opportunity to kill Hoyt, he hesitates. He only accomplishes the task because of taunting by the sheriff, but the gun was empty, so he didn't achieve his goal. Kemper dies because he is a less-than-ideal boyfriend. Erin wants to get married, and he claims that they will eventually, but they've been together for three years. His plan was to propose while at the concert, but it's too late, and he dies. He also lies to Erin. He told her they were going to Mexico for vacation, but they were actually heading down there to pick up marijuana.

The only death in *Texas* that seems out of place is the death of Andy. He fits into all the male stereotypes: he engages in sexual activity, which is socially acceptable for a male teen, and he helps Erin when she can't find Kemper. The only thing that is outside of social norms is his drug activity, which is part of the reason he is maimed. Andy isn't directly killed by Thomas, he is killed by Erin to end his suffering. While he pays for his drug use, he is a typical male, so Leatherface can't murder him for being outside of social stereotypes. By having Erin kill him, it shows both her compassionate side (feminine) and her do-what-has-to-be-done side (masculine). The scene is another way of showing how Erin is able to combine both masculine and feminine traits to survive.

In *Friday the 13th*, again, the characters are divided into their prospective gender categories. Amanda and Richie die after engaging in sexual activity. Amanda is the sexual aggressor, teasing Richie across the fire, which is unacceptable in female stereotypes. Richie's actions fall in line with a typical male teen, but, like Kemper, he is lying to his friends, which is also why Wade dies. The others believe they are in the woods to camp, but Richie and Wade are on the hunt for a marijuana crop. Chelsea and Bree die because they either engage in premarital sex, again as the sexual aggressor (Bree), or engage in activities that a stereotypical female wouldn't engage in, such as topless waterskiing (Chelsea). Jenna is the stereotypical female. She has long hair, she wears skirts, she is compassionate, and she doesn't engage in sexual activity or do drugs or drink. At first, it seems like she has all the makings of the Final Girl, but she lacks the ability to combine masculine traits with her feminine ones. She can't fight back and she can't protect herself, so she dies.

Chewie seems to be a typical male character—he likes to drink and likes girls—but he is shy when it comes to actually talking to girls, he's clumsy, and he drinks beer out of his own shoe, so he's disgusting. Lawrence doesn't seem to be too interested in the girls around him. He is more interested in smoking marijuana and masturbating while everyone else is busy. The farmhand is also interested in drugs and self-pleasure, so he doesn't fit into the stereotypes. Trent seems to fit the stereotypes: he has a girlfriend and he is attractive and wealthy. He is also a cheat and a liar, so he has to die. These characters can't mix their masculine traits with feminine ones, so they don't survive.

The first victim in *Nightmare* is Dean. He isn't onscreen for very long, so it's difficult to tell if he fits into his respective stereotype. He has a girlfriend, but he also has a lot of psychological problems that he is going to counseling for. A "real" male wouldn't need help dealing with his problems; he'd be able to take care of them on his own. The next victim is Kris. She is taken while lying in bed with Jesse. She has the traits of a stereotypical female: she has long hair, feminine clothes, and doesn't engage in sexual activity with Jesse. But she does allow him to sleep in her bed, and the implication is that she had sex with him previously. Jesse dies because he isn't masculine enough.

Like the originals, the killers are portrayed to be exceedingly masculine. However, like the originals, the killers have both masculine and feminine traits. Norman still dresses in his mother's clothes and has incorporated her personality into his. In *Black Christmas*, one of the killers is a woman, but she seems to have incredible strength since she can hoist dead bodies into the attic. Billy takes care to set up the murder victims around the Christmas tree so they can be a family, and he speaks in a female's voice on the phone.

Thomas Hewitt doesn't seem to have a feminine bone in his body. Unlike the 1974 film, he doesn't dress in women's clothes and serve the family dinner. He does, however, seem to have an unduly sensitive side. After all, the reason he started murdering was because other kids made fun of him.

In *Halloween*, like the original, Michael has moments of ambiguity. When the audience sees the scenes of him as a child, he seems to be androgynous: he has long hair and no defining masculine characteristics. He is sensitive and kind to his mother and baby sister, yet tortures and murders small animals. Even when he becomes an adult, his long hair is constantly in his face, and he hides behind a mask. While his strength and characteristics prove that he is male, he still retains his sensitive side for his sister.

Jason in *Friday the 13th*, like Leatherface, also seems to lack feminine characteristics. However, like Michael, he retains a sensitive side for his mother, which is why he doesn't kill Whitney. He also hides behind a mask. Freddy still sharpens his finger knives the way women file their nails, and his face has been altered to look more ambiguous. His burns function a lot like Jason's and Michael's masks—they make it difficult to see his real face.

The killers in slasher films have to be in the same in-between place as the teens or else they wouldn't be able to operate in the same space. However, they can't mix the masculine and feminine traits as well as the Final Characters. The masculine side always prevails, so they are defeated. Of course, they never stay down for long.

Be Able to Turn Expectations Upside Down

Another important aspect in the rites of passage is taking normal social expectations and turning them on their heads. In the original films, this was done from the very beginning of the film. Most of these movies were fresh ideas that had rarely been seen onscreen before. By the time the remakes were created, numerous films had been made and the films were losing their freshness. The challenge of the remakes was to take a story the vast majority of the population already knew and alter it just enough to be surprising, but it still had to stick true to the original story and turn social expectations upside down.

The remake of *Psycho* is almost an exact replica of the original, even down to the camera angles (see lesson 1 for an in-depth discussion on this topic). The 1998 version's changes include the movie being filmed in color and Lila being a little less passive (in the remake, she actually delivers the final kick that knocks Norman out and allows him to be captured).

Black Christmas sticks closely to the story about sorority sisters being murdered in their house near Christmas. The film opens up much like the original and focuses on the house, which is decorated with lights, while carols play in the background, and then the camera takes us into the house. Clair is sitting on the floor of her room wrapping presents when something in the closet draws her attention. For those audience members familiar with the original, they know the killer came out of the closet, so the film sets up certain expectations of how Clair will die. But the killer doesn't come out of the closet, and Clair goes back to what she was doing. When she sits back down, she looks for her pen, which is missing, and an unseen assailant throws a bag over her head. This scene is reflective of what happened in the original, and the audience expects certain things to happen. The film then defamiliarizes itself by having the killer stab Clair in the eye with the pen, something that never occurred in the original film. The scene then changes to a mental institution where the audience discovers Billy is being held. If he was the one who committed the original murders, who is killing the girls now? The audience finds themselves in unfamiliar territory. It also defamiliarizes the original story by giving the audience background on the killer. In the original film, the killer is shrouded in mystery. The only insight we have into why he killed was through his obscene phone calls, and that is cryptic. The remake takes the audience into his past and shows us what made him a murderer. It also adds two killers into the mix, making it hard for the audience to determine who will be the next victim and which killer will kill them.

The main elements from the 1974 version of *Texas* are still in the 2003 version with the teens traveling across the Texas countryside and getting slaughtered like cattle. Unlike the original, they aren't going to check on family graves, they are going to a concert, and the hitchhiker they pick up isn't part of the Hewitt family. The film defamiliarizes itself by having the hitchhiker kill herself in the back of the van and forcing the teens to find help. It also defamiliarizes itself by giving Leatherface a name, history, and family. While there was a family in the 1974 version, it was made up entirely of men. The remake adds females to the family, but they don't make the family sane. The expectation is that something terrible is going to happen to the teens, which the audience would know from the original. The teens still die, some in almost the same fashion as the teens in the original film. For example, when Andy is captured by Thomas, he is hung on a meat hook, just like Pam was. The film defamiliarizes itself when Andy doesn't actually die by Leatherface's hands; Erin has to kill him to put him out of his misery. Erin also has help, something Sally never had in the original. She wouldn't have been able to escape the basement without Jedidiah's intervention, but after that, survival is all up to her. Also unlike Sally, Erin is willing to fight against her killers—she doesn't just run and scream. By the end of the film, when the trucker has taken her back to the family, she takes matters into her own hands and steals the sheriff's cruiser, making sure to run over him in the process. While the ending is like the original and the Final Girl makes it to safety, it defamiliarizes itself because the Final Girl is not passive and she is able to destroy some of killers with her own hands.

Halloween, like the remake of *Black Christmas*, defamiliarizes itself by giving Michael an extensive past and letting the audience know exactly why he is killing. Laurie's character is changed just enough also to make things unfamiliar from the original. While she is still studious, a virgin, and responsible, she isn't a complete prude when it comes to sex. This is most evident when she teases her mom and makes sexual insinuations with a bagel. Annie also survives in the 2007 version. The end of the 2007 version also defamiliarizes itself from the original by having Laurie kill Michael. In the original version, she stabs him with a knitting needle and attempts to push him out the window, but Michael's ultimate defeat occurs when Dr. Loomis shoots him. At the end of the remake, Laurie delivers the final shot.

The remake of *Friday the 13th* opens with a scene of the past and a camp counselor killing Mrs. Voorhees. Jason watches from the woods, then goes to his mother's body and picks up a locket. This isn't a remake of the original *Friday the 13th*, in which Mrs. Voorhees was committing all the murders, but the members of the audience who were familiar with the original films would still understand the basic premise and know what to expect. The expectation the film sets up is that Jason will be killing teens, avenging his mother's death, and that is basically what happens. The film defamiliarizes itself by having Jason take Whitney as a prisoner. In the original films, he would have never let a teen survive, no matter how much they reminded him of his mother. In *Friday the 13th Part 2*, Ginny is able to distract Jason by acting like his mother, and he does hesitate killing her, but once he finds out she is just acting, he goes after her. In the remake, Jason knows Whitney isn't his mother but lets her survive anyway. The film also defamiliarizes itself by having Jason move quickly. In the original films, Jason never ran. He always attacked his victims with a slow, determined gait, and he was always successful in catching and killing them.

The opening of *Nightmare* shows us a group of people sitting in a diner. Dean is by himself at a booth, obviously very tired. He is drinking coffee, attempting to stay awake. When he falls asleep, he is tormented by Freddy. Dean wakes up just before something bad happens to him, and his girlfriend shows up to talk to him. Dean falls asleep again, and this time he doesn't get away from Freddy. In the original films, when Freddy killed someone in their sleep, the marks would just appear on their body. At the beginning of the 2010 version, it looks like Dean kills himself. This defamiliarizes the film because the other characters don't see the mystery in his death, the supernatural causes. Yes, they are upset about it and can't believe he did it, but they don't have any idea about Freddy until he starts showing up in their dreams.

The film also defamiliarizes itself by changing Freddy. He is still out for revenge and was still killed by the kids' parents, but instead of being just a child murderer, as he was described in the first film, he is now a child molester. In the first film, the teens never questioned his motives, they just knew he was a bad guy. But in the remake, they are led to believe that their parents might have gone a little crazy and killed an innocent man. Of course, this turns out to be false, and Freddy is just as evil and vile as the teens' parents claim him to be. The audience also gets a little more background. They are able to see Freddy interact with the kids at the day care and his reaction when the parents hunt him down and lock him in a boiler room. The scenes don't really add much to his history, but it does make the audience feel sorry for the guy. Like the characters, they begin to question whether or not he really was as bad as the parents claimed. This defamiliarizes it from the original because there was never any question about Freddy's evil in the first film.

Remakes have to remain true to the original films because they are a continuation of the franchise. There are certain expectations the audience has when they see the title and premise of the film. Elements within the film can be played with and changed to keep the film fresh and the audience from getting bored, and it can introduce a different history or explain the past of the killer in greater detail. Like the originals, the remakes take certain expectations and turn them on their heads, as expected in the rite of passage.

How to Survive

The teens in slasher films are supposed to be going through a rite of passage and learning the skills they will need to make it into the adult world. One of these skill sets is learning how to become a productive member of society, which is usually accomplished through a job. Since teens are outside of normal society and regular rules don't apply to them, this skill set is taught by combining work and play. Like the original films, the teens in the remakes who are able to mix these two skill sets are the ones who survive. (For a description of the combination of work and play in *Psycho*, refer to lesson 3.)

Kelli in *Black Christmas* is able to survive because she is the only sorority sister who has a job. She can't go home for the holiday because she has to work. Yet she also has a boyfriend, so she can combine the notions of work and play. The other girls come from privileged backgrounds, and the majority of them don't know the meaning of work or scoff when the idea is brought up. They play all the time, so they are killed. This is especially evident with Lauren. She is constantly drinking heavily and talking about the social injustices of the Christmas holiday. She doesn't even take responsibility for how much she consumes, so she throws up and has to be put to bed by one of the other girls.

Heather also has no sense of responsibility. The tradition in the house is to buy Billy a Christmas present, which they have been doing for several years. Heather draws his name for the secret Santa gift but doesn't like the tradition, so she decides not to participate. When she and Ms. Mac attempt to go to the police station to get help, Ms. Mac tries to hand Heather the window scraper to clean off the windows. Heather has no idea what it is or what it is used for, so she stays in the car while Ms. Mac does all of the work.

The deaths of the other sisters can be attributed to the same ideas. Leigh appears to be the person the sisters should strive to be: she seems to have passed the rite of passage into the adult world, and through her manner of dress, she appears successful. But, as the audience learns through her backstory, she might not be that responsible. She is divorced, so she couldn't make the relationship work; there are questions about whether or not she actually has a job; and she has just started to get to know her family again. Her sense of responsibility toward family and relationships is questionable, and she is so serious, it makes one wonder if she knows how to play at all. She dies because of her inability to mix work and play.

Erin is the responsible one in *Texas* because she doesn't do drugs or engage in questionable sexual behaviors. She has had the same boyfriend for three years. She is the only one who advocates loudly for the hitchhiker after she kills herself, and explains that the girl probably had a family who would want to know what happened to her. She puts Andy out of his misery when he is in the throes of death, and she rescues the baby from the Hewitt family. However, despite the sense of responsibility and duty, she is still able to have fun. The teens are traveling back from a vacation in Mexico and heading to a Lynyrd Skynyrd concert. Erin is looking forward to the music and talks about how she hopes the band will play certain songs. She survives because she knows how to mix responsibility and fun.

Kemper dies because of his inability to mix the two. He and Morgan have convinced the others to go to Mexico so they can pick up a large quantity of marijuana, which they plan to sell for profit. Instead of working hard for their money, they are going to get it by selling an illegal product. After the hitchhiker's suicide, Erin discovers their plan and gets angry at Kemper. At that point, he throws the piñata that hid the drugs into a field. He tries to be responsible, but by that time, it's too late. His sense of responsibility has already been clouded. The same thing can be said about marrying Erin. They have been together for three years and she has talked about marriage before, but he always tells her they don't have the money. She is all right with that and stays in the relationship because she loves him, but it is obvious the excuse is getting old. His plans are to propose to her at the concert, but the gesture is wasted. Again, his sense of responsibility comes in a little too late.

Andy is mainly concerned with instant gratification. When they pick up Pepper, she and Andy begin a sexual relationship without really knowing one another. They smoke dope and really don't seem to have any sense of responsibility at all. After all, Pepper was hitchhiking when they found her, which means she has no money and, more than likely, no job. She is traveling free across the country, counting on the goodwill of others to help her get by. Andy is like his friends and is content to take the income from the sale of drugs. He tries to be responsible by helping Erin find Kemper and heads to the Hewitts' house to look for him and find a phone. Like Kemper, by the time he finds a sense of duty, it is too late and he is killed.

Like the original, Laurie is a good example of how to combine work and play. She is a good student and takes her babysitting job very seriously. She even takes on Annie's child so Annie can have sex with her boyfriend. While babysitting, she still has fun with the kids, and teases Tommy about girls and the bogeyman. She watches TV with them, allows them to tickle her for a brief amount of time, then agrees to walk Lindsey home to ensure her safety.

The other teens in the film are killed because of their inability to mix these two traits. For example, Lynda never works. Even when it comes to cheerleading, instead of wanting to learn new cheers, she says something derogatory to the coach and gets kicked off the team. She hangs out with her boyfriend in an abandoned house drinking beer and having sex. She dies because she is unproductive.

Annie is attacked for the same reason. Instead of taking her babysitting job seriously, she pawns Lindsey off on Laurie so she can see her boyfriend. Unlike the original film, though, Annie isn't killed. She survives to be in the sequel, but she has been horribly scarred. Unlike Lynda, Annie isn't completely worthless when it comes to work. She knows what she has to do, and she is willing to do it, but she is also willing to play if given the opportunity. Also, unlike her character in the 1978 version, Annie doesn't smoke marijuana. There is still hope that she can become a productive member of society, so she is taught a lesson and her life is spared.

Whitney in *Friday the 13th* is also another good example of how to mix work and play. While talking to her boyfriend, she explains that she isn't very comfortable being in the woods; she thinks she needs to be home taking care of her mother, who is dying of cancer. Mike explains to her that her mother is the one who suggested that Whitney go camping, that she get out of the house and act like a normal teenager. After hearing that, Whitney is able to loosen up a little and enjoy the hike in the woods. Jason kills her friends but spares her life because of her sense of responsibility.

Clay is able to survive the ordeal because of his concern and duty to his sister. He is older than the teens, so he has a much deeper sense of responsibility and work ethic. His sister has been missing for six weeks, and he has spent the majority of that time traveling the county she disappeared in, looking for signs of her. He doesn't seem to play much, but he is willing to take Jenna's help. Even though he is still serious and looking for his sister, he is able to enjoy the woods with a nice girl. He would be the representative of the adult world that the teens are trying to mimic. He knows what has to be done to survive, especially since he left his house at seventeen, and his sense of duty to his family is unfaltering.

The other teens have no work ethic or sense of duty. Richie and Wade have brought everyone to the woods so they can find a crop of marijuana and sell it to make money. Amanda is only interested in sex. Mike almost seems like he can be responsible, but then he tells Whitney to take a locket they find in the dilapidated cabins. Since they have no sense of social obligations, they are killed.

When the new set of teens (Trent, Jenna, and their friends) show up to enjoy Crystal Lake, their lack of responsibility and work ethic becomes apparent. It begins in the gas station while the teens are on the way to the cabin. Trent and Jenna go into the station to pay for the gas and get some snacks, and Clay is in there talking to the attendant. He is asking the man if he's seen his sister, and wonders if he can place a flyer up in his store. Trent is impatient and rudely tells Clay to hurry up. After they leave and head to the cabin, it becomes readily apparent that Trent comes from a family with a lot of money. At first, it seems like Trent might be responsible. He tells his friends to be careful in the house and to not break anything. However, just the fact that he brought his friends there in the first place, more than likely without his parents' knowledge, is evidence of his irresponsibility. Then, he decides to cheat on Jenna with Bree, so he isn't able to combine the notions of work and play in a socially acceptable manner.

The other friends seem to have no respect for other people's belongings. Chelsea and Nolan take the boat out after Trent told them not to. Chewie is killed because he is constantly breaking things and drinking alcohol that doesn't belong to him. Lawrence is killed for doing drugs and disrespecting the house they are staying in. Bree has sex with Trent even though he isn't her boyfriend.

The only deaths that seem to be a little questionable in the film are Jenna's and the farmhand's. The farmhand seems to be able to mix the notions of play and work, so he should be safe from Jason's wrath. After all, the first time the audience sees him, he is busy putting wood through a chipper. However, he offers to sell Clay some marijuana, which taints the work ethic of doing honest work for an income. He also participates in socially unacceptable sexual practices, so he isn't a productive member of society.

Jenna seems to know how to mix work and play. When given the chance, she leaves her other friends so she doesn't participate in drinking or sex. She hangs out with Clay and tries to help him find his sister. She does have a sense of responsibility to help others in need. Since the audience doesn't know about her past, it's hard to explain exactly why she dies. It can be assumed that she probably comes from a privileged background, like her friends, so she might not have had to work for anything. This especially might be true since she goes tromping around the woods with Clay in sandals and a short skirt. Even though she is trying to act the part of being responsible, she doesn't really know how to go about it. However, this is all speculation since we don't have a clear picture of her past, but if she hasn't had to work for anything in her life, she wouldn't be a productive member of society and would have to die.

Nancy in *Nightmare* knows how to mix work and play. She is a good student, listens to her mother, has a job as a waitress, and is an artist. She gets all of her work done, then spends her evenings painting pictures and listening to music in her room. Quentin has the ability to be responsible, but he partakes in some actions that are questionable. For example, he knows that he and Nancy have to stick together to defeat Freddy. When she asks him to stay awake and watch her, he does. But he also stands up to his father and accuses him of killing an innocent man. He also steals Adrenalin from the hospital. Because of these actions, Quentin is horribly maimed by Freddy, but he isn't killed because the ability for him to become a productive member of society is there, he just needs to be taught a lesson.

As usual, the other characters die because of their inability to mix work and play. Kris is killed because she goes from boyfriend to boyfriend. At the beginning of the film, while Dean is sitting in the diner, a few tables away sit Jesse and his friends. They are talking about how Kris recently broke up with Jesse and started dating Dean. After Dean's funeral, Jesse goes to Kris's house to make sure she is all right, and she asks him to stay the night so she doesn't have to be alone. Freddy kills her in her sleep, and Jesse flees.

Jesse has no sense of responsibility because he is looking out for himself. He and his friends leave the diner when Kris enters because he is angry at her. After the funeral, while he seems to care that she is all right, his main objective is to get her back, to make himself happy. He flees the scene after Kris's death because he doesn't want to be accused of killing her, but his leaving actually makes him look more suspicious. He is killed after falling asleep in jail.

Even Nancy's mom becomes a victim of Freddy because of her inability to mix work and play. While it isn't important that she be able to mix them correctly since she's already passed the rite of passage, she does have a convoluted sense of responsibility. When the parents found out Freddy was abusing their kids, their first inclination was to make sure their children were safe, which is the right thing for parents to do. They didn't want the kids to endure the embarrassment of telling their stories to a jury, so they took justice into their own hands, which was not the right thing to do. They also denied the kids the ability to make their own decisions about how to feel about what happened in their past by taking the past away from them. While their intentions were in the right place, their actions went against normal social rules, so they are punished for it. Gwen actually loses her life, while the other parents are punished by having their children taken away.

Like the original films, sex also plays into the notion of work and play and separates the teens from adult world. Like the other aspects in the rite of passage, sex and sexuality create an in-between space for the teens to function in and allows them to explore themselves and others freely. Like the original films, sex in the teen world is set up to be fun, while sex in the adult world has become grotesque and uneasy.

This is especially evident in *Black Christmas*. The only teens in the film who actually engage in sexual activity are Megan and Kyle, and the audience only sees it after it has been recorded and posted on the Internet. It seems like this situation might be a little uneasy because Megan and Kyle have broken up and Megan is angry that the video has been posted for the world to see, but at the time of the act, she seems happy and having fun. Megan isn't upset that she engaged in sexual activity with Kyle; she is upset that it was filmed without her permission and then posted for others to watch. The actual act itself was fun, but the aftermath was detrimental. This ties into what is happening in the adult world in the film. The actual act of engaging in sex is fun, but the aftermath becomes detrimental, especially when the product is a child that has to be taken care of.

Billy's mother is unhappy with her offspring because of his appearance: he is yellow from a liver malfunction, and he reminds her of her husband. She shows her contempt for him by locking him in the attic and then by murdering his father with the help of her lover. But even after the father is gone, Billy's mother's life doesn't get much easier, and sex becomes work. She desperately wants to have another child, and she has sex with her lover to accomplish that, but he always falls asleep before he can ejaculate. Since he can't provide what she wants, she goes to Billy. She makes sex grotesque by creating a child with her own son.

In *Texas*, Andy and Pepper have just met one another, but they are attracted to each other and willing to explore each other's bodies. They don't actually engage in sex because there are other people around, but they do participate in a heavy make-out session. This relationship is fun for the two of them because they don't worry about disease, even after Morgan mentions the fact, and they don't worry about getting to know each other. They just worry about having fun and making each other feel good. This is juxtaposed with the Hewitt family. Here, the situation becomes grotesque and uneasy because of what happened to Thomas. As the offspring of a sexual encounter, his mother is obligated to take care of him. When he contracts a strange skin disease and parts of him fall off, she becomes overprotective. Kids made fun of him, so they were presumably killed. The family is so convinced that everyone who comes through their town is there to make fun of Thomas, they kill them, too. She cares for and nurtures Thomas, but that doesn't translate to the other children in the family. Jedidiah is forced to stay out with the dogs. When he asks nicely if he can come in, she gruffly tells him no.

Henrietta seems to be an ideal mother and takes care of what is believed to be her daughter. But, again, the situation becomes grotesque and uneasy. When Erin accidentally wakes the baby up, Henrietta grabs a can of beans out of the fridge to lull the child back to sleep. Then, Erin finds out that the child isn't even Henrietta's; it was kidnapped. The family doesn't know how to take care of their offspring, or has to take offspring from others, and they grow up to become killers. Erin is able to save the baby from a life of murder by taking her away from the family.

In *Halloween*, Deborah Myers is a stripper, so sex is no longer fun because it has become work. Her job also becomes grotesque and uneasy for Michael because bullies at school make lewd comments about his mother. He has an overwhelming desire to protect her, so he kills the bully. While Michael is in the asylum, the janitor brings in his cousin so they can rape a female patient. Not only do they rape the girl, they do it on Michael's bed. Sex here is grotesque and uneasy because of the invasive nature of the act. It isn't fun for the girl because she didn't consent, and Michael's space is being invaded.

It is questionable whether or not Laurie's parents ever engaged in sex for fun since they don't have biological children and her mother is a prude. While Laurie's father is talking about the hardware store owner, she mentions that he is a pervert. When her mother asks how she knows that, Laurie then proceeds to tell her that he is constantly staring at the girls and makes lewd gestures with a bagel. Sex becomes uneasy at that point because of the implications of child abuse. Laurie's mother becomes extremely upset with Laurie and hangs on to the hurt feelings all day. When Laurie comes home from school, her mother explains this to her and Laurie apologizes. After that, they drop the subject completely.

Also in *Halloween*, like the original, some of the parents don't have partners to engage in sex with. This is especially true for Sherriff Brackett and Dr. Loomis. It is obvious that Brackett had a partner at one time—he has a daughter—but what happened to her is unknown. Dr. Loomis even had a wife, but he devoted his entire life to Michael, so they divorced. Deborah did have a partner to engage in sex with, but he was wounded and covered in casts. He couldn't work, so Deborah had to supply the family with money. Since they have responsibilities to take care of, they have no time for fun.

There aren't a lot of adults in *Friday the 13th*. The few the audience sees onscreen is an old woman that Clay runs into while looking for his sister and the sheriff. The old woman warns him to leave well enough alone, then returns to her house and ignores him. The sheriff does the same. Clay has been in the county for six weeks and hasn't had any luck finding a trace of his sister. The sheriff tells him to do what the other families are doing and look elsewhere. The situation is grotesque and uneasy because the adult world is unwilling to help. The old woman knows what is going on, she knows about Jason, but she won't talk to Clay. The sheriff has exhausted all his leads, so he's just giving up.

In *Nightmare*, the notion of sex becoming grotesque and uneasy occurs when Freddy starts sexually abusing the children. The parents knew what was happening, and they tried to protect their children. They went so far as to kill Freddy in a boiler room just so their kids could avoid embarrassment. This leads to Nancy's mother becoming a single mother and Quentin's father looking untrustworthy. Even when Nancy's mother explains to Nancy and Quentin what happened, they don't believe it. They go out on their own and look for answers. However, when they find them, they find that their parents were right and the situation was worse than they could have imagined.

Not only is the adult world grotesque and uneasy, they are hung up on events from the past. There is a notion among the adults that all teens are exactly the same. This is true in *Texas* where Luda May believes all teens have come to town to make fun of her son, even when they didn't know he existed. It is true in *Black Christmas* when Billy and his sister kill the sorority girls to be a part of their family. They don't care where the girls came from, they just want their bodies around their tree. It is true in *Friday the 13th* when Jason is avenging his mother's death and will kill any teen who ventures close to his home, even though they had nothing to do with her death. All the kids in *Nightmare* had their past erased so they wouldn't have to remember the awful abuse they endured. The parents are so intent on keeping their children safe and keeping the memory of Freddy at bay, they don't give their children any way to protect themselves when he attacks.

The final step in the rite of passage is the reaggregation of the teens into the adult world. They were supposed to learn the skills that would allow them to function as adults, and the killers in slasher films were supposed to teach them those skills. The Final Characters in these films become reaggregated into society when they defeat the killer. This occurs because the Final Character is able to take the most dominant discourse in the film and make it her own. In essence, she is able to take the lesson she is being taught and apply it to her life. This happens in *Black Christmas* when Kelli shocks Agnes in the head with a defibrillator and kills her, and then when she pushes Billy over the side of a balcony and impales him on a Christmas tree. Erin in *Texas* becomes reaggregated into society when she attacks Thomas with a meat cleaver and then when she runs Sheriff Hoyt over with a car. In *Halloween*, Laurie shoots Michael with a gun. Clay fights against Jason in *Friday the 13th* and wraps a chain around his neck. When he becomes tangled in the wood chipper, Whitney seizes the moment to stab him with his machete. In *Nightmare*,

Nancy becomes reaggregated into society when she slices Freddy's throat with a blade from a paper cutter.

In slasher films, even though the teens are able to defeat the killer and use the dominant discourse of the film as their own, the audience rarely ever sees them actually make it back to society. The lessons the killers/teachers in slasher films teach them are not the lessons that are actually going to allow them to become functioning members of society. The lessons they are being taught are from a fictitious, idealized past. Plus, they never really defeat the killer, so the process is allowed to occur over and over again.

Conclusion

Teens are supposed to pass from childhood into adulthood, and their elders are supposed to teach them the proper way to achieve that goal. There is a specific process and certain phases in a rite of passage a teen has to go through if he or she is going to make it to the adult world. These include separating from society, negotiating gender, and turning normal expectations upside down. The teachers in slasher films are the killers, and their lessons are from an idealized, fictitious past. The teens don't want to be a part of that society, so they fight against and defeat the teacher. The goal of the teens is to enact social change. However, like the originals, this doesn't translate over to society as a whole because the majority of the teens are dead, and we never see the Final Characters make it back to society. In essence, these films don't portray how well the rites of passage work, they show how they have failed. For the audience watching these films, there is a lesson there, and they have to figure out what to change to ensure harmony.

THOSE WHO IGNORE HISTORY ARE DOOMED TO REPEAT IT: SLASHER REMAKES

It can be debated whether or not Hollywood has run out of original ideas. Many films that have come out in theaters recently have been remakes of earlier films. But it must be stressed that Hollywood is a for-profit business. They want to ensure they will make money, and it is easier to do that with a film that has already been made than by taking a chance on an original story. In many cases, this is why slasher films are remade. Most original slasher films were made on a limited budget but saw huge returns when the films went to the theater. It's possible the studios are hoping the same thing will occur with a remake, but that rarely happens.

The remakes of slasher films attempt to remain true to their original roots, but they change a few elements to keep the audience interested in the films. Most of the new elements incorporate the use of better graphics to show the murders, more graphic murder scenes, and perhaps adding even more murders. One of the things the remakes try to remain true to are the themes that define these films. However, they may make the traumatic events that shaped the killers more clear or delve more deeply into their past, emphasizing the need to create an idealized past.

Retraumatizing the Killer

The 1998 version of *Psycho* is almost an exact copy of the original film. It uses the same sets, dialogue, and camera angles. Like the first, the emphasis in this film is on the desire for women to return to the home. This is done through the characters of Marion and Sam and through Norman and his mother. Since the film is exactly like the original, refer to lesson 1 for a discussion on these topics.

The 1998 version attempts to take us a little deeper into Norman's mind. It focuses more on his mature desires, such as when he is watching Marion through the hole in the wall. It is more apparent in the 1998 version that he is aroused by her actions and masturbating while he watches her than in the 1960s version. He then proceeds into the house and sits at the table, resting his head in his hands, apparently feeling guilty about or ashamed of what he just did. While Lila is going through the Bateses' house, she goes into Norman's room. It is decorated as if a young boy still lives there. Stuffed animals sit on the bed, army men are arranged on the desk, and toys line the shelves. Yet, she finds a pornographic magazine among the toys. Norman's desire to return to the past is emphasized in his room. He still wants to believe he is the little boy his mother used to take care of, but he can't escape the fact that he has grown into an adult and has adult desires. Although it is not out of the realm of possibility for a young child to have a porn magazine in his room, it seems even more out of place sitting on the shelf. Most children try to hide that kind of thing from their parents out of fear they will get caught and punished, but this is out in the open, emphasizing the fact Norman has grown up.

The desire to return to the past is impossible, which is constantly emphasized throughout the film. Marion wants to return to Phoenix to make amends, but she is murdered before that can happen. Norman wants to return to a time when he was cared for by his mother, but she is a rotting corpse and he has grown up. Again, the 1998 version of the film also emphasizes how destructive the past was. Norman's mother was still overbearing and clingy, and what is Marion going to return to? She will still be unmarried and, more than likely, unemployed. The desire for both of these characters to return is so strong, it destroys them. For Marion, she is killed, and for Norman, he experiences a psychotic break. By the end, Norman doesn't even have control of his own thoughts anymore; the mother part of his brain has completely taken over. Like Marion, he has ceased to exist.

Unlike in the original film, the killer in the 2006 version of *Black Christmas* gets a history and a name. The film also adds the twist of having two killers instead of one. Like in the original film, the family in the 2006 version has fallen apart. The girls that are left in the sorority house are there because they have nowhere else to go or because their family doesn't want them around. But even in their makeshift family, they can't get along and are constantly arguing. The killers murder them and pose them in the attic around the Christmas tree so that they can be a part of their family.

In the case of the killers, the reason they murder the sisters is to have them function as family members. In the context of the film, the traumatic event that defines the killers revolves around the fact that the biological family has become violent and murderous. In the case of Billy, his mother hated his father, and when he was born, all she saw was her husband in the baby, so she separates herself emotionally and physically locks Billy in the attic. The only person who shows Billy any type of love is his father, but it's evident he can't stand up to his wife, and, eventually, he is killed by his wife and her lover. The family breaks down even further when Billy's mother sexually abuses Billy and he fathers a child with her. Once Agnes is born, Billy is left out of the picture entirely. He eventually gets his revenge on Christmas and kills his stepfather and mother, making it a point to cut the flesh out of his mother's back with cookie cutters and eats it as the cops show up. He attempts to murder Agnes, but only succeeds in gouging out her right eye. She was sent to the orphanage, but since no one wanted her, she returned home and began murdering the sorority sisters.

Both Billy and Agnes know only violence when it comes to their family life. Billy was abused by his mother and witnessed the death of his father, while Agnes was brutally attacked by her father/ brother. After the murder of his mother, Billy was committed to an asylum, and his only desire is to return home. The security guard explains that every Christmas he attempts to escape. Since Agnes doesn't know any different, either, she also returns to the house, awaiting the return of her father/brother. They kill the girls and make them a part of the family because they don't know any other way to show their love.

The killers desire to return to a past when the family was intact, but for Billy, that time never existed and he took it away from Agnes. The notion of family and love has become distorted, and the only way the killers can get it back is by murdering the sisters around them. Kelli knows what it is like to be in a loving family, even though she can't be with them. She fights and defeats the killers because she doesn't want to return to their version of the past or be a part of their family.

The focus of the 2006 version of *Black Christmas* is the same as the 1974 version: the desire to return home. The majority of the sorority sisters are getting ready to spend Christmas with their families, with the exception of the few that are left behind. These sisters don't enjoy celebrating the holiday or being around their families. In one instance, while talking about burying the hatchet with family members and spending time with them, Dana mentions that she would like to bury the hatchet with her sister, "Right in her head." Lauren makes it a point to let everyone still at the house know exactly how she feels about Christmas and its pagan origins and its overcommercialization, all the while drinking way too much and spouting off curse words. Even Clair, who is getting ready to go home and get to know her sister, seems to have issues. She has to open a bottle of wine and struggles to write a card to her sister, but she doesn't have to worry for long because she is the first to die.

It is evident in the 2006 version that the nuclear family has completely disintegrated. However, both Kelli and Leigh desire to have a family. Kelli is an only child and wants nothing more than to have a sister, which may be the reason she joined the sorority. When the murders occur, her desire is to make sure everyone stays together for safety. Since she doesn't realize the girls are actually dead yet, she also wants to find the missing girls. When Ms. Mac and Heather want to go to the police station to find help, Kelli doesn't want to leave the others behind. Leigh comes to the house looking for her sister, Clair, and refuses to leave without knowing what happened to her. She claims that they didn't have a close relationship, but they were trying to amend that. When Leigh, Kelli, and Kyle discover the girls might be dead, Leigh and Kelli want to head up to the attic to make sure. Kyle doesn't think it's a good idea, but Kelli comments that if she had a sister, she would expect her to look for her. When Kyle says she doesn't, Leigh retorts that she does now. At the end of the film, while Kelli is laid up in a hospital bed, Leigh opens her Christmas present in front of her, commenting that Clair can't be there to watch. Since their real families can't be around, they replace them with people who care about them, like a normal family should.

Kelli survives the encounter with the Lenz family because her desire for family is pure. She is considerate and kind to the other sisters in the house, even though they may be rude to her. She realizes that families fight and don't get along, and she is willing to take the good with the bad. But she also knows that the sorority sisters can never actually replace her real family. She desires to be with them for the holidays, but her responsibilities at work keep her at the house. She tries to stay calm when the murders start happening and tries to keep the sisters together. The other sisters are murdered because they don't know how to act in a family.

Unlike the first film, there are really no indicators of why the family in *The Texas Chainsaw Massacre* is killing. It is kind of implied and assumed that it is because the slaughterhouse has been closed down, but there is no concrete evidence. Leatherface, who is no longer referred to as Leatherface but has a name, Thomas Hewitt, still kills his victims as if they are cows, and the teens pass a sign on the side of the road advertising BBQ. However, there is also the indication that the teens are being killed for actions instigated by a previous generation. When Erin escapes the clutches of Thomas, after Pepper has been killed with a chain saw, she runs to a trailer in the woods looking for help. The women in the house cryptically refer to some child who had a skin disease who the other kids made fun of. After Erin passes out from being drugged and regains consciousness in the Hewitt house, Luda May stands at the ironing board, again saying something about how she knows why the teens came to the town; that they came like all the others to make fun of her boy.

The implication here is that Thomas/Leatherface has been the butt of jokes from the time he was a child until the present. The desire of the family is to protect their child, and they appear to do this by killing the perceived threats. For the family, this may have included the original teens who made fun of him (that is unclear), but it also includes any outsider that may venture into town.

As is typical of slasher films, the desire is to return to a time of the nuclear family. As is also typical of slasher films, the movie shows how this ideal is fictionalized and never really existed. It juxtaposes the teen generation against the "ideal" generation to show the differences between the two, but it also emphasizes how corrupt the notion of the nuclear family has become. In the 1974 version, there weren't any women in the family at all, so there was no way the family could propagate. In this version, there are women, but they are just as psychotic as the men. For example, when the teens arrive in town with the body in the back of the van, they enter the store where Luda May works. Most normal people would react in some way to seeing a dead body, but Luda May acts as if it's an everyday occurrence. She even charges the teens for use of her phone. Granted, she is surrounded by the rotting flesh of pigs and cows, but a human being should be different. The teens find out much too late that Luda May is in cahoots with the killers.

When Erin comes across the mobile home in the woods, a typical reaction would be for the women to wonder what in the world is going on. After all, Erin was pounding on the door frantically, and upset and crying about being chased. Instead, their reaction is very calm and they offer her tea. Again, Erin finds out too late that the women are involved with the family.

There is evidence that the Hewitt family is a complete family with children and grandchildren, but who the parents of those children are is unclear. While they are very concerned with how Thomas is treated and make sure no one makes fun of him for his skin disease, it is also apparent they don't take care of their other offspring. In one particular scene after Erin has been captured, Jedidiah asks if he can come in the house. His grandmother firmly tells him no and that he has to stay out with the dogs. However, Henrietta has kidnapped a child from a family they slaughtered, and they completely dote on her.

The Hewitt family is supposed to represent the ideal family: there is a mother, a father, and children, as well as grandchildren. The teens are supposed to represent the downfall of the nuclear family. They believe in free love and will have sex with anyone they pick up, which is evident in how Pepper and Andy are all over each other in the back of the van. Erin has been living with her boyfriend for three years outside of wedlock. However, the ideal family has degraded into murder and refuses to take care of their own. Like the 1974 version, this could be due to the fact that the slaughterhouse has closed down and left them to rot, or it could be because of how society has tormented and teased Thomas. What exactly happened to the family is unclear.

Sheriff Hoyt also represents how the past has become idealized and fictionalized. After the girl kills herself in the back of the van, Erin and Pepper want to turn her over to the authorities instead of dumping her on the side of the road. They claim she has parents out there somewhere who deserve to know what happened to her. Little do they know, her parents have already been killed. The sheriff is supposed to be the ultimate figure of social authority. He is supposed to be the embodiment of their morals and ideals and punish those who step outside of the boundaries. At first glance, Sheriff Hoyt does represent those traits. He assists the teens in getting the body out of the van and wonders what they are doing. However, it doesn't take long for the audience to see that his actions are slightly odd, such as when he talks about groping the corpse or having the teens put her in the trunk so he doesn't get blood in his patrol car. The whole notion of having to meet the sheriff at an abandoned mill also seems suspicious.

Later, after Erin and Andy head back to the house to find Kemper, the sheriff comes back. Again, at first, he seems like the representative of society's morals. When Erin shows up hysterical and screaming about how Andy was murdered, he tries to calm her down. He then notices the remains of a joint in the ashtray. He makes the teens lie down in the dirt while he inspects the van. He then begins to torture them by making Morgan climb into the van and show him exactly what happened when the girl shot herself, which includes sitting in the blood and bits of gore left on the seat.

It is evident that Morgan is scared to death of the sheriff. Even though the teens were trying to do the right thing, the killer traps them and tries to blame them for other things, such as smoking marijuana or engaging in sexual behavior. The death no longer becomes the focus, but what the teens may or may not have been doing in the van becomes top priority. To further emphasize how corrupted society has become, the sheriff hands Morgan a gun and tells him to reenact the suicide. Morgan points the gun at the sheriff and pulls the trigger, symbolizing the teen generation's desire to enact social change and the lengths they will go to accomplish it, but the killer isn't stupid, and he isn't going to give the teens a loaded weapon. Again, the killer is trying to lure the teens into a situation that goes against social norms and then punish them for it. Morgan is hauled off in handcuffs, but he isn't taken to jail. The sheriff drives him to the Hewitt house, where he becomes another victim.

Like the first film, the 2003 version of *Texas* focuses on hippies. The characters are driving across Texas in a van, and the majority of them dress from that era. Unlike the first film, their conversations do not focus on the alignment of the stars. In the new film, there is more of an emphasis on sex and drugs. As they cruise down the highway, two people are making out in the back, breathing heavily and ignoring the three other people in the van. The audience finds out a short while later that the girl is a hitchhiker the teens picked up a few days earlier. The hippie generation practiced and preached the idea of free love and experimented with sex, regardless of how well (or how little) they knew their partner. This scene reinforces their ideals. The two finally stop kissing and pawing one another when Morgan points out the statistics of kids their age getting a sexually transmitted disease. They then proceed to roll and light up a joint, which is passed around the van until it falls into the hands of Erin, who throws it out the window. It is after this that the audience finds out the group has just been in Mexico and picked up a piñata full of marijuana. This upsets Erin, who obviously wants nothing to do with the drug.

The rest of the film deviates from the 1974 version because the group is not checking to make sure family graves are still intact, they are traveling to a Lynyrd Skynyrd concert. As they continue on their way, they almost run over a girl as she walks down the middle of the road, and they pull over to make sure she is all right. It is obvious she is in distress, so they put her in the van. They keep their distance from her, keeping her on one side while they stare at her from the other. She starts mumbling about how "he was a bad man," and then freaks out when they pass the slaughterhouse. Shortly after that, she pulls out a gun and kills herself. The teens are obviously upset and freaked out about the whole situation. They want to do the right thing, so they find a store and call the sheriff. Little do they know, the town they stopped in is run by the Hewitt family and they have no intention of letting the teens go.

Erin, the Final Girl, tries to follows society's rules and do the right thing by reporting the suicide. When Morgan is in the van with the sheriff and she sees Morgan pointing the gun at him, she tries to convince him not to do it. Her only desire is to go home. Sadly, because society has been corrupted and is intent on destroying the teen generation, or at least forcing them to follow their rules, no matter how insane they are, any of her actions, even those done with good intentions, will draw unwanted attention. This is why she gets captured and has to fight against the killers.

The remake of *Halloween* returns to Michael's childhood to give the audience insight into why he does what he does. This return to his childhood is also a return to the family, which is the desire in the film. Yet, as can be expected, this return is not the ideal, conservative past the killer wants to return to. Michael has two parents present, but the father is not his biological father, and he is cruel and mean to him. His mother is kind and caring, but she is also a stripper. He has two sisters, one who is older and a narcissist, and the other is a baby who has no idea what is going on. His mom and stepdad are constantly arguing, and he spends his time in his room, killing his pet rats.

Michael's family life is bad, and his social life is nonexistent. He is a loner who doesn't have any friends and is picked on by bullies. Eventually, he just snaps and kills people, starting with the bully and then moving on to his family. The only two people who seem to be immune to his wrath are his mom and baby sister. After being placed in the mental institution, his mother and Dr. Loomis try to hold up the illusion of family. Michael has no memory of the murders, and at one point asks how everyone at the house is doing. Instead of Deborah (his mother) telling him they are all dead, she just says that everything at the house is fine.

His mother visits him every week and they eat together, and Dr. Loomis even becomes a surrogate father figure. As time progresses, Dr. Loomis joins them for meals. There is a sense of normalcy and family togetherness at a dinner with Dr. Loomis, Michael's mom,

A loving and devoted mother (Sheri Moon Zombie) with her son, Michael (Daeg Faerch), in *Halloween* (2007). *Dimension Films/Photofest © Dimension Films*

and Michael while music plays, but the situation is tense. No one talks. Michael's mother tries to lighten the mood by bringing Michael a picture of himself and his sister, but it doesn't break the silence. Later, after his mother and Dr. Loomis have left, the nurse makes a comment about the picture, and Michael murders her with a fork.

Treatment for Michael does not work, and he slips further and further into his own mind, to the point where he refuses to speak or remove the masks he creates. Dr. Loomis has tried to help him, but he can't. He feels like he has failed. After fifteen years, he decides that it is time to move on, telling Michael that he has become like his best friend after all these years and he feels responsible for him, like a father would. But unlike a father, since he was unable to fix Michael's problems, he walks away. It is interesting to note that after all the horrific things Michael did to his family, his mother still came to visit him. He murdered his sister and his stepdad, yet she still loved him and wanted to him to get better. When she realizes he isn't going to get better, she too abandons him by committing suicide. By this point, Michael has nothing left. He seems to be content living his life in his cell making masks, until the outside world comes barging in. He uses the opportunity to escape and heads back to Haddonfield to find his family.

Michael's dysfunctional life is juxtaposed against Laurie's idyllic life. She lives in a house with two parents who love her, and she doesn't seem to worry about anything. She is a good student and a responsible teenager. When the audience first meets her and her family, her mother is cooking eggs and her father is running around the house looking for his glasses. This scene is a mirror image of the scene when we first meet Michael's family. His mother, too, is at the stove cooking eggs, but his stepdad is at the table covered in casts. While Laurie's mother is helpful and shows her husband where his glasses are, Michael's mother verbally chastises her husband for not working. The worst thing that happens in Laurie's house is she teases her mother about the local hardware store owner, claiming that he is a pervert and making lewd gestures with a bagel. Michael's house is a different story: his stepdad makes comments about how sexy Michael's sister is before pushing everything off the table onto the floor and then making Deborah clean it up, as well as the verbal abuse, the teenage sex (Michael's sister), and the murders.

Michael wants to return home. When he is young and in the mental institution, he is always asking when he can go home. When he gets out, it is the first place he goes. His desire is to have his family back, but since the only family he has known was abusive, he brings murderous actions with him. He tries to reunite his family by bringing in his mother's grave, substituting Lynda's body for his sister, and by bringing Laurie back into the house. However, since returning to the past is impossible and Laurie has no idea what is going on, Michael is destroyed.

Laurie was part of the Myers family, but she was young enough that she doesn't remember it. Like everyone else in the town, she knows about the events that occurred on that Halloween day, but she doesn't talk about them. When Michael comes back and tries to return, Laurie doesn't understand what he is trying to return to. Her past has been hidden from her, and she is content not to go back there. She fights violently against Michael and eventually ends up defeating him because she doesn't want to be a part of his version of the past.

The remake of *Friday* is not a remake of the first *Friday the 13th*, but of part 2. The killer in the 2009 version is Jason, not his mother. However, like the original, the traumatic event that shaped Jason into a killer was watching his mother get beheaded on the shore of Crystal Lake. He develops a desire for revenge and takes it out on teens who venture into his domain.

The focus in this film, like so many other slasher films, is the desire for the return of the family. As the opening shows, Jason's mother killed the counselors to avenge the death of her son. When she is killed on the bank of the lake, Jason wants so badly to avenge his mother's death, he returns from the dead to finish the killings she started. Whitney wants to return to her mother, because she feels guilty for leaving when she was sick. After Whitney winds up missing, Clay, her brother, shows up to find her, hoping to reunite the family.

The notion of family is much more pronounced in the 2009 version than the original. After Mrs. Voorhees is killed, Jason makes it a point to retrieve a locket from her body. In it, there are pictures of him and her. He takes the trinket back to the cabins at Crystal Lake and keeps it in a safe place. When Whitney and Mike come to the cabin to explore, they find the locket. After opening it, Mike comments that the picture looks like Whitney, and he tries to convince her to keep it. Jason attacks a while later, and Mike is killed. Whitney heads back to the camp to find her other friends have already been murdered. The scene cuts away just as Jason raises his machete over his head while going after Whitney.

Later in the film, the audience finds out that Jason has spared Whitney and chained her up in his house, which is a series of tunnels under the summer camp. The implication is that Whitney really does look like his mother and his desire to have his family back is so great that he will chain up a victim to hang on to the illusion of his mother. Despite his killing tendencies, he won't do anything to hurt Whitney. His attachment to Whitney is further emphasized at the end of the film. Clay and Jason are fighting, and it's pretty obvious Clay isn't going to win. Whitney is able to distract Jason by acting like his mother. She calls out his name with authority, and when he turns around, she is holding out the locket. Jason stops, believing his mother is talking to him, and this gives Clay enough time to wrap a chain around Jason's neck and defeat him.

Clay's desire to find his sister also reinforces the ideal of family. Like Jason, Whitney and Clay have lost their mother, who died from cancer. According to Clay, Whitney was her primary caretaker, who spent every moment next to her taking care of her. When she didn't show up at the funeral, Clay knew something was wrong. He travels to her last known location and refuses to believe she can't be found. She has been missing for six weeks, and even though they didn't get along very well in the past, he still feels the need to find her and make sure she is safe.

Whitney's desire to escape from Jason's clutches doesn't appear to come into play until Clay shows up. While the audience can't know this for sure because we don't see what she has been doing, it is evident that she doesn't fight back until Jason attacks her brother. Until that point, she is content to hide and cower from the killer. Clay is knocked unconscious while they are escaping through an overturned bus, and Whitney hides from Jason, but instead of being passive, she actually attacks and kicks him in the face. During the final confrontation in the barn, after Clay has wrapped the chain around Jason's neck and thrown it into the wood chipper, Whitney delivers the final strike with Jason's machete, plunging it into his chest.

The desire in the film is to return to a time when the family was intact. Clay and Whitney are able to survive because they know they can't change the past. They know that they can't bring their mother back. Clay also explains to Jenna that he wasn't a very good brother. He left home when he was seventeen and didn't look back. The last time he talked to his sister was six months prior to his looking for her, and they argued on the phone. However, both Whitney and Clay are able to recognize that wrongs occurred in the past and move beyond them. They don't dwell on what happened but focus on what they need to do. Jason is unable to do that. He still tries to live in the past, to avenge his death and his mother's murder, even if it means taking out his wrath on teens who had nothing to do with either, which is why he is able to be defeated.

Like the original *Nightmare*, the traumatic event that shaped Freddy into a murderer was being burned alive in a boiler room by vengeful parents. Also like the first film, the emphasis in the 2010 version is the desire to return to innocence. However, none of the teens in the movie remembers being young. The parents in the film don't want the kids returning to the past. In the context of the film, something very awful and detrimental to their upbringing occurred, so the parents erase their children's memories and get rid of any evidence from their childhoods. The teens are content and don't wonder about their childhood until Freddy starts attacking; then the teens become curious about what happened.

The desire in the film is the return to innocence, but the teens never had an innocent childhood. Since they were five or six, they were subjected to a pedophile, who may or may not have sexually abused them. Like the first film, Freddy attempts to get revenge for what the parents did to him. Also like the first film, when justice cannot be served by society, the parents take it into their own hands. They then try to hide what they did from the kids, hoping it will allow them to grow up untraumatized.

When Freddy returns to kill the teens in their sleep, he brings with him the desire to know about the past. He shows them snippets of their childhood, just enough to pique their interest. The teens take the bait and start poking around and questioning what happened when they were kids. They soon learn the past is subjective and experienced differently by everyone. Freddy wants the teens to believe that what happened to him was done out of spite, and he wants to turn the teens against their parents. He presents to the teens a past that was full of wonderful memories and friends. The teens don't remember that they had all known each other when they were little. They think they just met when they got to high school. But Freddy lets them know that they had wonderful times together while attending a day care. They would still have those wonderful memories if it weren't for their parents.

At first, his plan works, and the teens look at their parents with suspicious eyes. Due to their prodding, Quentin and Nancy find out where the day care was located and who Freddy was. Nancy's mother also informs them he abused them, and tells them stories of how they would come home with marks on them or with stories about his secret cave. Yet they never had enough evidence to take to the police, so the parents took matters into their own hands. This doesn't sit well with Quentin and Nancy. In one scene, Quentin argues with his father, demanding to know why they didn't go to the police. His father attempts to defend his position, but Quentin refuses to hear it. Quentin comments that they were only six, they could have made anything up, reinforcing that he believes Freddy never hurt any of the kids.

The teens don't remember the past, and they are willing to believe Freddy's version of it because it seems plausible. Since most teens naturally rebel against their parents and rules, Freddy's past gives the teens the perfect opportunity to distrust the older generation. As they continue to poke and prod into history, they discover their parents had been right and Freddy was just as evil and sexually abusive as they said he was. By this point, though, the teens can't ask their parents for help, they have to save themselves.

The teens don't necessarily desire to return to innocence; they are just looking for answers. They know they are different from their peers, but they don't know why. In the beginning, they are content living in their ignorance, but as time goes by and their friends start dying, the desire to know about the past becomes overwhelming. As they start digging into their past and learning the truth, the notions of innocence and whatever ideals they believed in are shattered.

Freddy is supposed to represent the conservative past. He is supposed to represent a time when children obeyed authority figures without question. But in the context of the film, this ideal past never existed. The authority figures were either sexually abusing the children or trying to cover up the truth.

Freddy wants to return to the past, when the children were innocent, not only to punish the parents for what they did to him, but for his own desires. This is evident when Nancy has gone into the dream world to defeat him, and she finds herself clothed in a white dress that she used to wear as a child. Freddy even comments how it used to be his favorite. By the time she is in that dress, she remembers everything that happened to her, everything that Freddy did to her. However, Freddy's fantasy cannot last because Nancy is no longer a little girl and they cannot return to the past. Like other slasher films, the teens do not want to return to the idealized past, they want to create their own social changes. This is evident in the way Nancy fights back.

Freddy decides he wants to toy with Nancy a bit, so he tosses her around the room. While feigning injury, Freddy moves closer, and Nancy stabs him in the eye with a pair of scissors. Since they are in the dream world, Freddy can't be hurt, and he throws Nancy back onto the bed. He tells her that he wanted her to be the last one awake so she would be so tired she would never wake up. What Freddy doesn't count on is that Quentin actually does his job and wakes Nancy up by stabbing a needle of Adrenalin into her heart. She pulls Freddy into the real world, and is able to defeat him with the blade of a paper cutter. To show how badly she doesn't want to return, she first cuts off the hand with the knife glove, representing how powerless his weapons are in her world, then she kills him by slitting his throat.

The 2010 version of *Nightmare*, like the original, is lacking a nuclear family, especially fathers. The one father that is present is Alan Smith, Quentin's father, and he was the instigator in Freddy's death. There appears to have been fathers present before Freddy was killed, but what happened to them after is a mystery. By 2010, the definition of a "family" has changed exponentially, and the notion of nuclear families has become obsolete. Unlike the original *Nightmare*, the Final Girl, Nancy, doesn't want or expect her father to save her. In the first place, he isn't even around, and she doesn't mention him. She knows that if she is going to defeat Freddy, she has to do it herself. She asks Quentin to help her, and, like the original, it seems like he is going to fail like Glen. But he is able to wake back up and plunge a needle into Nancy's heart at the right moment. He is also able to keep Freddy occupied long enough in the real world for Nancy to pick up a sharp blade and defeat him.

Again, like the original, the parents were only trying to protect their children. Their desire was to retain the innocence of childhood by not making their kids take the stand in court and tell everyone what Freddy did to them. They tried to bury the past, but the past always has a way of coming back. In this case, it came back in the form of Freddy, and he wasn't going to stop until the truth was known and his vengeance was fulfilled. The Final Characters are able to survive their ordeal with Freddy because they don't operate within his rules and boundaries. Even though they learned the truth about their past, they weren't constrained by it.

The film itself refers back to the past by copying scenes from the 1984 version. This is evident in Kris's death, which is very similar to Tina's. Kris is dragged up the wall and torn to shreds while her boyfriend, Jesse, looks on. He then takes off running, much like Rod did in the original. Jesse becomes the major suspect and is arrested. Like Rod, he is then murdered while in jail. The film also pays homage to the original *Halloween*, which is evident near the end of the film when Nancy tries to capture Freddy. While being chased, she hides in a closet, much like Laurie did while hiding from Michael. Unlike

Halloween, Nancy doesn't stab Freddy in the eye with a hanger. He is able to get into the closet with her, and she runs for her life.

The 2010 version of *Nightmare* returns to the past to reference the 1984 version, but it also changes the story to appeal to new audiences. The 1984 version of the film was very popular and grossed a lot of money. By mimicking those scenes, the film hopes to appeal to the audience members who may have watched the original version, but it also knows that it can't reproduce the movie in its entirety and be successful. Since returning to the past is impossible, the makers of new version have to take from the original and create something new, something slightly different, and hope that it will be successful.

How to Survive

Surviving in the remakes is just the same as surviving in the originals. Final Characters have to recognize the danger they are in and fight against it. They have to have some of the conservative traits the killer finds ideal. But most important, they have to be able to stand up to the killer. They have to be able to take the killer's murderous desire to return to the past and use it against him, thus guaranteeing themselves a future.

Lila in the remake of *Psycho* is just like Lila in the original, although not quite as passive. She possesses conservative ideals such as not engaging in premarital sex or stealing like her sister, but she is also outspoken and refuses to believe the explanations she's given about her sister. She ventures into Norman's house and finds his mother's corpse, and even though Sam still saves her at the end, unlike the original Lila, the 1998 Lila delivers a kick that knocks Norman out while he is struggling with Sam. This action guarantees that Norman can be taken into custody.

Kelli in *Black Christmas* is virtuous and has a work ethic. She cares about the other girls, even when they are mean and nasty to her. She has a boyfriend, but the audience never sees them engage in sex onscreen. There are indications that they might not be at that stage in their relationship, which is evident while kissing in the car. Kyle definitely wants to take things further, but Kelli tells him she's not ready. Later, Megan (another sorority sister) sits at her computer watching a video. She becomes visibly upset, and the audience learns she is watching a sex tape of Kelli and Kyle. Obviously, Kyle enjoys engaging in sexual practices, but he doesn't force Kelli to do anything she doesn't want to.

Kelli also has a good work ethic. While the other sisters are getting ready to head home and be with families they don't enjoy being with, Kelli is stuck at the house because she has to work. Both of these traits would fit with the killers' conservative ideals and fictitious past, and that is why Kelli is able to fight against them. Both killers still attempt to kill her, but she has the ability to fight back.

Erin in *The Texas Chainsaw Massacre* has lived with her boyfriend for three years and, more than likely, engaged in sexual acts with him, but the audience never sees it onscreen. She desires to get married, and mentions it while in the van, but is also content just being with Kemper because she loves him. She doesn't do drugs. When given the opportunity, she throws the joint out the window. She's also very caring and refuses to leave the suicidal girl's body on the side of the road. It is the caring and loving traits that save her against Thomas. While trapped in the basement, she tries to help Andy down from the hook he's been hung on, but she isn't strong enough. Instead of letting him suffer, she puts him out of his misery by stabbing him to death. As Thomas steps down the stairs to dispatch her, Jedidiah helps her escape. From there, she's able to recognize the trouble she's in and fights against it, saving the baby the family kidnapped in the process.

Laurie was Michael's baby sister in *Halloween*, but she was lucky enough to have no memory of the dysfunction that turned Michael into a killer. Adopted by a loving family, she grows up to be virtuous and trustworthy. Like the original Laurie, the remake Laurie doesn't have a boyfriend, although she's interested in boys, and she takes her babysitting duties very seriously. Her actions are the opposite of the actions of Michael's older sister, and that's what saves her. Michael wants to have his family back, and he spares Laurie's life. However, since she doesn't realize he is her brother, and he's killed her friends and family, she fights against his desires. After struggling and hiding from Michael, she finally gets the upper hand and is able to shoot him in the face. However, she doesn't come out of the ordeal unscathed, and it's obvious by the end of the film that she's been altered by the experience.

Whitney in *Friday the 13th* is very caring and uninterested in sex. She feels bad for going on the camping trip because she believes she needs to be by her sick mother's side. When Mike, her boyfriend, tells her that her mom wanted her to come, she feels a little better but never comfortable. Like other Final Girls, Whitney doesn't engage in sex onscreen. While the other couple fulfills their desires, Whitney and Mike take a walk, stumbling across the decrepit Camp Crystal Lake. Jason attacks, but he doesn't kill Whitney. Instead, he takes her prisoner because she reminds him of his mother. She recognizes the danger the teens are in. She is also able to fight against and kill Jason.

Nancy in *A Nightmare on Elm Street* knows she's different from her friends. Partly it's because of what Freddy did to her, but it's also because she has conservative traits. She's the only one the audience sees working, and she refrains from being involved with boys. She was Freddy's favorite when he was molesting the children, but that only gives her a reason to fight harder against him at the end.

Conclusion

The remakes of slasher films focus on the same thing as the originals: the desire of the killer to return to a conservative, fictitious past that he has created. It shows how destructive this desire to return can be. The remakes also show how impossible this return is and focus on how the ideal pasts never existed. To accomplish this, the lives of the killers are explored in more depth, and the illusion of a conservative, ideal past full of nuclear families and teens who didn't question authority is shattered.

BIBLIOGRAPHY

Clover, Carol J. *Men, Women, and Chain Saws: Gender in the Modern Horror Film*. Princeton, N.J.: Princeton University Press, 1992.

Deflem, Mathieu. "Ritual, Anti-Structure, and Religion: A Discussion of Victor Turner's Processual Symbolic Analysis." *Journal for the Scientific Study of Religion* 30, no. 1 (1991): 1–25.

Dika, Vera. *Games of Terror:* Halloween, Friday the 13th, *and the Films of the Stalker Cycle*. London: Associated University Presses, 1990.

Engel, Jeremy. Written By. "Timeline of Terror." October 1998. www .wga.org/WrittenBy/1098/Timeline.html.

Fletcher, Angus. *Allegory: The Theory of a Symbolic Mode*. Ithaca, N.Y.: Cornell University Press, 1964.

Heba, Gary. "Everyday Nightmares: The Rhetoric of Social Horror in the *Nightmare on Elm Street* Series." *Journal of Popular Film and Television* 23, no. 3 (Fall 1995): 106.

imdb.com. "*Black Christmas* (1974)." www.imdb.com/title/tt0071222/.

———. "*Black Christmas* (2006)." www.imdb.com/title/tt0454082/.

———. "*Friday the 13th* (1980)." www.imdb.com/title/tt0080761/.

———. "*Friday the 13th* (2009)." www.imdb.com/title/tt0758746/.

———. "*Halloween* (1978)." www.imdb.com/title/tt0077651/.

———. "*Halloween* (2007)." www.imdb.com/title/tt0373883/.

———. "*A Nightmare on Elm Street* (1984)." www.imdb.com/title/ tt0087800/.

———. *"A Nightmare on Elm Street* (2010)." www.imdb.com/title/tt1179056/.

———. *"Psycho* (1960)." www.imdb.com/title/tt0054215/.

———. *"Psycho* (1998)." www.imdb.com/title/tt0155975/.

———. *"Scream* (1996)." www.imdb.com/title/tt0117571/.

———. *"The Texas Chain Saw Massacre* (1974)." www.imdb.com/title/tt0072271/.

———. *"The Texas Chainsaw Massacre* (2003)." www.imdb.com/title/tt0324216/.

Infoplease.com. "1950–1999." www.infoplease.com/ipa/A0903597.html.

Mack, Carol K., and Dinah Mack. *A Field Guide to Demons, Fairies, Fallen Angels, and Other Subversive Spirits.* New York: Henry Holt, 1998.

Phillips, Kendall R. *"The Exorcist* (1973) and *The Texas Chainsaw Massacre* (1974)." In *Projected Fears: Horror Films and American Culture.* Westport, Conn.: Praeger, 2005.

———. *"Halloween* (1978)." In *Projected Fears: Horror Films and American Culture.* Westport, Conn.: Praeger, 2005.

Pinedo, Isabel Cristina. *Recreational Terror: Women and the Pleasure of Horror Film Viewing.* Albany: SUNY Press, 1997.

Rockoff, Adam. *Going to Pieces: The Rise and Fall of the Slasher Film, 1978–1986.* Jefferson, N.C.: McFarland, 2002.

Sharrett, Christopher. "The Idea of Apocalypse in *The Texas Chainsaw Massacre*" in *Planks of Reason: Essays on the Horror Film.* Edited by Barry Keith Grant. Metuchen, N.J.: Scarecrow Press, 1984.

Turner, Victor. *From Ritual to Theatre: The Human Seriousness of Play.* New York: Performing Arts Journal Publications, 1982.

———. *The Ritual Process: Structure and Anti-Structure.* New York: Aldine De Gruyter, 1995.

Washer, B., and B. O'Brien. 2004. Friday the 13th: The Website. www.fridaythe13thfilms.com.

Wikipedia. "1949." en.wikipedia.org/wiki/1949.

———. "1957." en.wikipedia.org/wiki/1957.

———. "1958." en.wikipedia.org/wiki/1958.

———. "1959." en.wikipedia.org/wiki/1959.

———. "1963." en.wikipedia.org/wiki/1963.

———. "1970." en.wikipedia.org/wiki/1970.

———. "1973." en.wikipedia.org/wiki/1973.

———. "1974." en.wikipedia.org/wiki/1974.

———. "1975." en.wikipedia.org/wiki/1975.

———. "1980." en.wikipedia.org/wiki/1980.

———. "1982." en.wikipedia.org/wiki/1982.

———. "1984." en.wikipedia.org/wiki/1984.

———. "1991." en.wikipedia.org/wiki/1991.

———. "1996." en.wikipedia.org/wiki/1996.

———. "1997." en.wikipedia.org/wiki/1997.

———. "1998." en.wikipedia.org/wiki/1998.

———. "Feminist Movement." en.wikipedia.org/wiki/Feminist_movement.

———. "*Friday the 13th* (2009 Film)." en.wikipedia.org/wiki/Friday_the_
13th_ (2009_film)#Plot.

FILMS CITED

Abrams, Barry. *Friday the 13th*. DVD. Paramount, 1980.

Bayer, Samuel. *A Nightmare on Elm Street*. DVD. New Line Cinema, 2010.

Carpenter, John. *Halloween*. DVD. Anchor Bay Entertainment, 1978.

Clark, Bob. *Black Christmas*. Film Funding Ltd. of Canada, 1974.

Craven, Wes. *A Nightmare on Elm Street*. DVD. New Line Cinema, 1984.

———. *Scream*. DVD. Dimension Films, 1996.

Hitchcock, Alfred. *Psycho*. DVD. Shamley Productions, 1960.

Hooper, Tobe. *The Texas Chain Saw Massacre*. DVD. Vortex, 1974.

Marcus, Adam. *Jason Goes to Hell*. DVD. New Line Home Entertainment, 1993.

Miner, Steve. *Friday the 13th Part 2*. DVD. Paramount, 1981.

Morgan, Glen. *Black Christmas*. DVD. Dimension Films, 2006.

Nispel, Marcus. *Friday the 13th*. DVD. New Line Cinema, 2009.

———. *The Texas Chainsaw Massacre*. DVD. New Line Cinema, 2003.

Van Sant, Gus. *Psycho*. DVD. Universal, 1998.

Zombie, Rob. *Halloween*. DVD. Dimension Films, 2007.

APPENDIX:
LIST OF SLASHER FILMS

Friday the 13th **Franchise**

Friday the 13th. 1980. Directed by Sean S. Cunningham.

Friday the 13th Part 2. 1981. Directed by Steve Miner.

Friday the 13th Part III. 1982. Directed by Steve Miner.

Friday the 13th: The Final Chapter. 1984. Directed by Joseph Zito.

Friday the 13th: A New Beginning. 1985. Directed by Danny Steinmann.

Friday the 13th Part VI: Jason Lives. 1986. Directed by Tom McLoughlin.

Friday the 13th Part VII: The New Blood. 1988. Directed by John Carl Buechler.

Friday the 13th Part VIII: Jason Takes Manhattan. 1989. Directed by Rob Hedden.

Jason Goes to Hell: The Final Friday. 1993. Directed by Adam Marcus.

Jason X. 2002. Directed by James Isaac.

Freddy vs. Jason. 2003. Directed by Ronny Yu.

Friday the 13th. 2009. Directed by Marcus Nispel.

A Nightmare on Elm Street **Franchise**

A Nightmare on Elm Street. 1984. Directed by Wes Craven.

A Nightmare on Elm Street 2: Freddy's Revenge. 1985. Directed by Jack Sholder.

A Nightmare on Elm Street 3: Dream Warriors. 1987. Directed by Chuck Russell.

A Nightmare on Elm Street 4: The Dream Master. 1988. Directed by Renny Harlin.

A Nightmare on Elm Street 5: The Dream Child. 1989. Directed by Stephen Hopkins.

Freddy's Dead: The Final Nightmare. 1991. Directed by Rachel Talalay.

Wes Craven's New Nightmare. 1994. Directed by Wes Craven.

Freddy vs. Jason. 2003. Directed by Ronny Yu.

A Nightmare on Elm Street. 2010. Directed by Samuel Bayer.

Psycho **Film Series**

Psycho. 1960. Directed by Alfred Hitchcock.

Psycho II. 1983. Directed by Richard Franklin.

Psycho III. 1986. Directed by Anthony Perkins.

Bates Motel. TV. 1987. Directed by Richard Rothstein.

Psycho IV: The Beginning. 1990. Directed by Mick Garris.

Psycho. 1998. Directed by Gus Van Sant.

The Psycho Legacy. 2010. Directed by Robert V. Galluzzo.

Scream **Film Series**

Scream. 1996. Directed by Wes Craven.

Scream 2. 1997. Directed by Wes Craven.

Scream 3. 2000. Directed by Wes Craven.

Scream 4. 2011. Directed by Wes Craven.

The Texas Chainsaw Massacre Franchise

The Texas Chain Saw Massacre. 1974. Directed by Tobe Hooper.

The Texas Chainsaw Massacre 2. 1986. Directed by Tobe Hooper.

Leatherface: The Texas Chainsaw Massacre III. 1990. Directed by Jeff Burr.

Texas Chainsaw Massacre: The Next Generation. 1994. Directed by Kim Henkel.

The Texas Chainsaw Massacre. 2003. Directed by Marcus Nispel.

The Texas Chainsaw Massacre: The Beginning. 2006. Directed by Jonathan Liebesman.

The Texas Chainsaw Massacre 3D. 2012. Directed by John Luessenhop.

The following lists other slasher films, but it is not exhaustive or all-inclusive. I'm sure I forgot many, but this gives you an idea of the vast amount of slasher films out there.

Alone in the Dark. 1982. Directed by Jack Sholder.

April Fools. 2007. Directed by Nancy Norman.

April Fool's Day. 1986. Directed by Fred Walton.

Black Christmas. 1974. Directed by Bob Clark.

Black Christmas. 2006. Directed by Glen Morgan.

Blood Night: The Legend of Mary Hatchet. 2009. Directed by Frank Sabatella.

The Burning. 1981. Directed by Tony Maylam.

Cheerleader Camp. 1988. Directed by John Quinn.

Cherry Falls. 2000. Directed by Geoffrey Wright.

Christmas Evil (a.k.a *You Better Watch Out*). 1980. Directed by Lewis Jackson.

The Dorm That Dripped Blood. 1982. Directed by Stephen Carpenter and Jeffrey Obrow.

The Driller Killer. 1979. Directed by Abel Ferrara.

Drive-In Massacre. 1977. Directed by Stu Segall.

Final Exam. 1981. Directed by Jimmy Huston.

Girls Nite Out. 1982. Directed by Robert Deubel.

Graduation Day. 1981. Directed by Herb Freed.

Grizzly Park. 2008. Directed by Tom Skull.

Happy Birthday to Me. 1981. Directed by J. Lee Thompson.

Hatchet. 2006. Directed by Adam Green.

Hellbent. 2004. Directed by Paul Etheredge.

Hell Night. 1981. Directed by Tom DeSimone.

Holla. 2006. Directed by H. M. Coakley.

Hospital Massacre. 1982. Directed by Boaz Davidson.

The House on Sorority Row. 1983. Directed by Mark Rosman.

Humongous. 1982. Directed by Paul Lynch.

I Know What You Did Last Summer. 1997. Directed by Jim Gillespie.

The Initiation. 1984. Directed by Larry Stewart.

The Legend of Bloody Jack. 2007. Directed by Todd Portugal.

Madman. 1982. Directed by Joe Giannone.

Mother's Day. 1980. Directed by Charles Kaufman.

My Bloody Valentine. 1981. Directed by George Mihalka.

My Super Psycho Sweet 16. TV. 2009. Directed by Jacob Gentry.

New Year's Evil. 1980. Directed by Emmett Alston.

Night School. 1981. Directed by Ken Hughes.

Prom Night. 1980. Directed by Paul Lynch.

The Pumpkin Karver. 2006. Directed by Robert Mann.

Savage Weekend. 1979. Directed by David Paulsen.

Scream Bloody Murder. 1973. Directed by Marc B. Ray.

Silent Night, Bloody Night. 1974. Directed by Theodore Gershuny.

Slash. 2002. Directed by Neal Sundstrom.

Slaughter High. 1986. Directed by George Dugdale, Mark Ezra, and Peter Mackenzie Litten.

Sleepaway Camp. 1983. Directed by Robert Hiltzik.

Slumber Party Massacre. 1982. Directed by Amy Holden Jones.

Splatter University. 1984. Directed by Richard W. Haines.

Student Bodies. 1981. Directed by Mickey Rose.

Terror Train. 1980. Directed by Roger Spottiswoode.

The Toolbox Murders. 1978. Directed by Dennis Donnelly.
Urban Legend. 1998. Directed by Jamie Blanks.
Valentine. 2001. Directed by Jamie Blanks.
Visiting Hours. 1982. Directed by Jean-Claude Lord.
Wrong Turn. 2003. Directed by Rob Schmidt.

INDEX

Note: Page numbers in italics refer to photographs.

Brackett, Annie, of *Halloween*. *See* Annie, of *Halloween*

Brackett, Sheriff. *See* Sheriff Brackett

Braun, Jesse, of *A Nightmare on Elm Street* (2010). *See* Jesse, of *A Nightmare on Elm Street* (2010)

Bree, of *Friday the 13th* (2009), xix, 123, 154, 164

Brenda, of *Friday the 13th* (1980), xix, 58, 76, 82, 95

brothers, xviii, 25, 45, 56, 72, 75, 96, 139–40, 152, 176, 185–87, 193

Burrel, Jack, of *Friday the 13th* (1980). *See* Jack, of *Friday the 13th*

camera work, xiii, 117, 156, 157, 174; first-person camera, 21, 22, 41, 86, 91; first-person perspective, xix; killer's perspective, xiii; point-of-view shots, xvi; subjective camera, xiii; subjective point of view, xiii

Camp Crystal Lake, xiv, xix, xx, 13, 15, 50, 78, 88, 103, 106

cannibalism, 127, 132

Caroline, of *Psycho* (1960), 6

Casey, of *Scream*, xxiv, 37, 75, 79, 91

chain saw, xi, xxv, 26, 38, 52, 57, 92, 107, 125, 135, 136, 138, 177

change, 142, 143; in killer, 112, 114, 115, 117

Chelsea, of *Friday the 13th* (2009), xix, 122, 154, 164

Chewie, of *Friday the 13th* (2009), xix, 122, 154, 164

child molestation, 113, 117, 118, 135, 159, 167, 169, 175, 187–88, 193

child murder, xxii, 18, 159

childhood: of killer, xviii, 7, 111, 115, 126, 133, 147–48, 155, 157, 158, 160, 173, 177, 182, 184; of victims, 15, 18, 25, 68, 107, 123, 126, 130, 134, 141, 187–89

Chris, of *Black Christmas* (1974), xvii, 9, 10, 99, 103

Christmas, xvii, xviii, 9, 84, 113, 118, 119–20, 126, 131, 138, 146, 157, 175–77

Christy, Steve, of *Friday the 13th* (1980). *See* Steve, of *Friday the 13th*

Clair, of *Black Christmas* (2006), xviii, 119, 129, 153, 157, 176, 177

Clare, of *Black Christmas* (1974), xvii, 7–10, 22, 47, 52, 66, 71, 74, 77, 80, 84, 91, 99, 103

Clay, of *Friday the 13th* (2009), xix, xx, 119, 123, 124, 129, 140–41, 142, 143, 163, 164, 165, 170, 185–87

clothes, as a sign of gender, 26, 41, 60, 79, 81, 142, 150, 154, 155

Clover, Carol, vii–viii, 70, 71, 73, 75, 81

Colvin, Leigh, of *Black Christmas* (2006). *See* Leigh, of *Black Christmas*

ABOUT THE AUTHOR

Jessica Robinson has a master's in English from the University of Wyoming and writes freelance science articles, as well as horror and science fiction under the pen name of Pembroke Sinclair. A former staff writer for *Serial Killer Magazine*, she works as a technical editor for an environmental consulting firm and as a freelance editor for several publishing houses. Her story "Sohei" was named one of the Best Stories of 2008 by the *Cynic Online Magazine*, and her novels *Coming from Nowhere* and *Life after the Undead* can be found through her website at pembrokesinclair.blogspot.com.